What to Eat

Before, During,

and

After Pregnancy

What to Eat

Before, During,

and

After Pregnancy

Judith E. Brown,

R.D., M.P.H., Ph.D.

McGraw·Hill

New York   Chicago   San Francisco   Lisbon   London   Madrid   Mexico City
Milan   New Delhi   San Juan   Seoul   Singapore   Sydney   Toronto

The McGraw-Hill Companies

Library of Congress Cataloging-in-Publication Data

Brown, Judith E.
      What to eat before, during, and after pregnancy / by Judith E. Brown.— Rev. ed.
         p.   cm.
   Rev. ed. of: Nutrition and pregnancy. Los Angeles : Lowell House, ©1998.
   Includes bibliographical references and index.
      ISBN 0-07-145921-9
      1. Pregnancy—Nutritional aspects.   I. Brown, Judith E. Nutrition and pregnancy.
  II. Title.

   RG559.B758   2006
   618.2′42—dc22   2005032435

1 2 3 4 5 6 7 8 9 0   DOC/DOC   0 9 8 7 6

ISBN 0-07-145921-9

Interior design by Andrea Reider

McGraw-Hill books are available at special quantity discounts to use as premiums and sales promotions, or for use in corporate training programs. For more information, please write to the Director of Special Sales, Professional Publishing, McGraw-Hill, Two Penn Plaza, New York, NY 10121-2298. Or contact your local bookstore.

The information contained in this book is intended to provide helpful and informative material on the subject addressed. It is not intended to serve as a replacement for professional medical advice. Any use of the information in this book is at the reader's discretion. The author and publisher specifically disclaim any and all liability arising directly or indirectly from the use or application of any information contained in this book. A health-care professional should be consulted regarding your specific situation.

This book is printed on acid-free paper.

Behind every advance in knowledge that leads to improvements in quality of life are individuals who, without benefit to themselves, volunteer to take part in research studies. Here's to the women who participate in research that advances our knowledge about nutrition and fertility, pregnancy, and breast-feeding. You benefit our children and all of us. This book is dedicated to you.

≈ Contents ≈

⌒ Foreword ⌒

Pregnant women have always accepted the importance of good nutrition, and health professionals are finally realizing just how important it is for pregnancy, as well as fertility and breast-feeding. In the last ten years, there has been a veritable explosion of books, pamphlets, and guides for pregnant women. In most cases, information prepared by professionals has been either too technical or too impersonal for the general public. At the other extreme, popular books prepared for the layperson have tended to lack enough scientific credibility.

In *What to Eat Before, During, and After Pregnancy*, Judith Brown fulfills her intention of writing a readable, useful, and accurate guide that is both upbeat and supportive in tone. Essential topics are covered with sufficient detail, helping women make the right choices about diet, supplement use, weight gain, and infant feeding.

With its combination of impeccable accuracy and positive emphasis, this book will be a major influence in helping women become nutritionally prepared for conception, pregnancy, and breast-feeding.

Howard N. Jacobson, M.D.
Professor, Dept. of Community and Family Health
College of Public Health, University of South Florida

⟿ Preface ⟿

Looking for reliable information about preparing your body for pregnancy? Is it taking longer than you had hoped to become pregnant? Are you pregnant and concerned that you may be gaining too much weight, or are you unsure about which foods and supplements you should consume and which you should avoid? Do you need to know about nutrition for twin pregnancy? Are you anticipating a need for facts about breast-feeding or getting your body back into shape after your baby is born? If questions and concerns like these brought you to the bookstore or library, you have found the right book.

Plenty of sources of information about nutrition and fertility, pregnancy, and breast-feeding are available, but the quality of the information varies from outlandish to great stuff. *What to Eat Before, During, and After Pregnancy* presents science-based information that is as reliable as it gets. This feature qualified past editions for reference use by physicians, nutritionists, midwives, nurses, and journalists. Updated information printed here delivers the same quality of information and practical advice.

Chapter 1 first provides an overview of the benefits of good nutrition for pregnancy, then addresses the role of nutrition in fertility and how changes in diet and exercise can increase your chances of becoming pregnant. Chapter 2 covers basic information on nutrition, including facts about vitamins and minerals and their leading food sources. Specific nutrition tables presented here are referred to throughout the book.

Perhaps the greatest advances in our knowledge about nutrition and reproduction in the past ten years have been made in the areas of preconceptional and early pregnancy nutrition. Chapter 3 highlights these advances, giving specific recommendations on optimal nutrition for early fetal development and growth and providing instructions on how to evaluate your diet.

Chapter 4 describes "the right diet for pregnancy" and answers questions about diet during this time. The pros and cons of using vitamin, mineral, and herbal supplements during pregnancy and indications for their use are covered in Chapter 5.

Weight gain during pregnancy has important influences on fetal growth and development and on body weight after pregnancy. Chapter 6 covers this topic and includes a weight-gain graph that can be used to monitor progress. Nutritional recommendations for women "eating for three" are also covered. Notes to women bearing triplets are also given, but this information is quite tentative because appropriate studies are yet to be done. Closely aligned with weight gain is the topic of exercise, so Chapter 7 explains the whys, hows, and benefits of exercising during pregnancy.

Pregnancy has a number of "side effects" that would be considered abnormal in women who are not pregnant. These common and bothersome problems can sometimes be effectively prevented or managed with changes in diet, exercise, or the use of supplements. Chapter 8 covers nutritional aids for nausea and vomiting, heartburn, and constipation. Background information and nutritional recommendations for conditions that arise during pregnancy, such as gestational diabetes, preeclampsia, and iron deficiency anemia, are also covered in this chapter.

The next two chapters address postpregnancy topics. Chapter 9 includes infant nutrition and feeding recommendations. Chapter 10 is devoted to the topic of breast-feeding.

I encourage readers to peruse Chapter 11. The recipes for healthy eating have been created specifically to help women meet nutritional needs before, during, and after pregnancy. Nutrition information is provided for each recipe.

Literally thousands of research reports and other sources of dependable information about nutrition and fertility, pregnancy, and breast-feeding were used during the development of this book. Because space considerations preclude listing them all, only key references and those to which women may wish to refer for additional information are included. Particularly good Internet and other resources related to topics covered appear at the end of the book, listed by chapter.

Throughout this book, women are referred to as the primary audience. This is because women are in the best position to act upon the information. Clearly, spouses, partners, in-laws, and grandparents-to-be may be interested in these topics and provide much valued support. Reference to women is not meant to exclude other interested or involved individuals.

Knowledge about maternal nutrition is continuously expanding, and new, important developments may not be addressed here. For this reason, and because new information may affect the type of health care you receive, you are urged to keep your health-care provider informed about your understanding of new developments and about your concerns and actions related to diet, supplement use, and weight. It is entirely possible that your inquiries will help update your health-care provider on important developments in nutrition.

Best wishes for good humor, happiness, and a bundle of joy.

⌒ Acknowledgments ⌒

I feel a deep indebtedness to those who have directed my interest toward producing that ounce of prevention worth a pound of cure. My daughter Amanda and my son Max piqued my interest in this area. I have learned many lessons about the nutritional ounce of prevention from Agnes Higgins, the former director of the Montreal Diet Dispensary; Howard Jacobson and Charles Mahan, obstetricians who promote prevention; and Sally Lederman of Columbia University, who is a crystal-clear thinker about evidence related to nutrition and pregnancy outcome. I have been given the opportunity to learn about nutrition and pregnancy and to write, teach, and consult about what I learned by grants from the National Institute of Child Health and Human Development, the Centers for Disease Control, and the Maternal and Child Health Bureau of the Public Health Service. My primary instructors, however, have been and will remain those wonderful women who volunteered to participate in our research studies.

This edition of *What to Eat Before, During, and After Pregnancy* (previously titled *Nutrition and Pregnancy*) includes a new group of recipes that are nutrient based. They're dishes I make frequently but hadn't written down before. Hugs and kisses to family and friends who tested the recipes and provided valuable feedback: Amanda Cross, Doug Wickman, Dr. Susan Brown, Don Hildebrand, Barbara Ellington, Helen Martens, and Bonnie Bernstein. Dr. Bea Krinke, a longtime friend, colleague, and expert cook, provided a large measure of helpful advice and analyzed many of the recipes for nutrient content.

～ 1 ～

Giving You and Your Baby the Nutritional Advantage

"Enormous amounts of information are barreling down the information highway, but they are not arriving at the doorsteps of our patients."

—Claude Lenfant,
National Institutes of Health Director

Today we are experiencing an explosion in new information about nutrition and fertility, pregnancy, and breast-feeding. A renaissance in research is underway, and it is redefining what nutritional advice should be given to women who are attempting to conceive or who are pregnant or breast-feeding. Advice previously based on clinical assumptions or personal biases is being replaced with recommendations supported by solid evidence. There are important advantages to the scientifically supported recommendations that are emerging from today's studies: They have been demonstrated to benefit health and they hold up over time.

It wasn't that long ago that nutritional factors were regarded as being unrelated to fertility. We now know that antioxidant intake; body fat stores; supplement use; and conditions such as insulin resistance, polycystic ovary syndrome (PCOS), and celiac disease all influence fertility. It used to be thought that the fetus was a parasite, extracting from the mother whatever nutrients it needed for growth and development regardless of the mother's diet. (Some people still believe this is true today.) It is now accepted that the fetus is not a parasite; it does not benefit while harming the mother. Nourishment of the fetus depends on the supply of nutrients from the mother's diet and her nutrient stores. To ensure survival of the species, it is the mother who gets primary access to most nutrients if nutrient supply is low. A healthy mother can reproduce again.

In the past, women were said to have maternal instincts that would direct them to select and consume nutritious foods during pregnancy. This notion is as valid as the ancient Roman belief that if you wanted a child with dark eyes you should eat mice often. Other common ideas, such as the recommendations that all women limit exercise, be wary of caffeine and diet soda, restrict their salt intake, and diet to keep their weight low in pregnancy, are no longer supported. Contrary to the opinions of some, the nutritional and health advantages of breast-feeding are not restricted to women with perfect diets, breast size, or health status.

New information about nutrition and fertility, pregnancy, and infant feeding emerges constantly, and it is difficult for health-care providers to stay current with all of the advances. Unfortunately, many providers are not up to date on the low-tech, nondrug nutritional improvements that could benefit women and the families they serve.

How Nutrition Can Affect Your Baby's Health

Much of the earlier advice given to women about nutrition and reproduction was insufficiently supported by scientific research and heavily biased by unproven assumptions. As knowledge expands, so should the specific recommendations given to women about nutrition. Some advances in nutrition information slowly seep into health care; others seem to be kept secret. A number of nutritional measures can be undertaken to enhance the chances of conception for many women and to increase fertility in men. It is also clear that a growing and developing fetus is vulnerable to the influence of energy and nutrients it receives from the mother and that excessive vitamins and minerals from supplements may be as hazardous to fetal well-being as deficient amounts. It is now known that a woman's intake of certain vitamins, such as folic acid, vitamin A, and vitamin D, very early in pregnancy can be related to the development of certain malformations in the baby. How much weight women gain in pregnancy and the timing of the gain have important effects on the risk of preterm delivery and the size and health status of infants at birth.

One of the most striking advances in research concerns maternal nutrition and the subsequent risk of certain chronic diseases. It appears that a predisposition for heart disease, diabetes, high blood pressure, and a number of other diseases and disorders may be "programmed" by inadequate supplies of energy or nutrients during gestation and early infancy. A large body of evidence indicates that well-nourished newborns with optimal growth may be at lower risk for developing a wide variety of health problems later in life.

Right next to this advance in terms of importance is new knowledge about nutrient-gene interactions. Genetic makeup is rarely the sole factor influencing health or disease risk. Rather, health and health problems tend to result from interactions among multiple genetic and environmental factors, such as dietary intake. Nutrient-gene interactions during pregnancy, for example, influence a woman's risk of developing gestational diabetes, her requirement for folate (a B vitamin), and how susceptible a fetus is to the effects of maternal alcohol intake. These advances are particularly exciting because we can modify dietary intake and environmental exposures in ways that benefit long-term health.

Well-nourished women are less likely to experience miscarriages or to develop iron deficiency anemia, constipation, fatigue, and other common problems of pregnancy. Babies born to well-nourished women are more likely to be born in robust health, to feed vigorously, to grow optimally, and to be alert and responsive. Although there is much more to be learned about the effects of nutrition on fetal growth, development, and subsequent health, the influence of maternal nutrition is being recognized, and the advantages of optimal nutrition are more extensive than previously imagined.

How Nutrition Can Affect Your Fertility

The conception and the delivery of a healthy baby are influenced by many conditions that are both within and outside of our control. Of those within our control, nutrition is primary. The type of diet a woman consumes before and during pregnancy can influence fertility and pregnancy in multiple ways. Under the right circumstances, good nutrition can be a gift, an above-average start on life and health advantages that last for a lifetime.

Conception results from a carefully orchestrated chain of biological events. Given the complexity of the processes involved, it is amazing that conception ever occurs! Remarkably enough, conception occurs without a hitch in nine out of ten couples. For one in ten, however, there's a glitch. The cause can be abnormal sperm, tubal disease, hormone irregularities, advanced age, or something unknown. The cause of the glitch can also be related to nutrition.

The list of nutritional factors related to infertility in both men and women now includes:

- Body fat
- Disorders, such as PCOS and celiac disease, related to the body's utilization of nutrients
- Nutrient intake
- Extremely high levels of physical activity
- Excessive caffeine or alcohol consumption

Infertility related to nutritional factors can almost always be managed by low-tech solutions. As a bonus, new research shows that certain dietary habits, weight status, vitamins, minerals, and certain herbs can have a positive effect on restoring fertility. Although nutritional approaches will not prevent or restore fertility in everyone, they represent safe, healthful, low-cost, and underused potential solutions for many couples.

Body Fat and Fertility

Infertility due to or aggravated by nutritional factors is often related to changes in hormone production or activity, or sperm quality. For nutritional problems related to hormone production or activity, the broken link can be repaired in as little as a month. It takes seventy-two days for sperm to be produced. Consequently, nutritional changes introduced will take at least seventy-two days to affect sperm quality.

Estrogen is a hormone that plays a major role in reproduction in women. It is produced in two places in the body: the ovaries and fat stores. Low or high levels of body fat and a tendency to store fat centrally (around the waistline) all change estrogen production. These modifications in estrogen production can lead to infertility or a delay in conception due to a loss of menstrual periods, irregular periods, or a lack of ovulation (egg release). The amount and location of body fat may also alter the production of other reproductive hormones in ways that decrease fertility and increase the risk of miscarriage.

A number of studies have demonstrated a normalization of reproductive hormone levels and a correction of infertility after body fat content is brought closer to the normal range. Weight loss as modest as fourteen pounds among obese, infertile women, through a reduction in caloric intake and an increase in physical activity, has been shown to correct infertility in a majority of women studied. Weight loss generally reduces central body fat stores and lessens the risk of infertility and delayed conception related to a waistline pattern of fat storage. On the other hand, modest amounts of weight gain in women with too little body fat can enhance fertility. Although drugs can be used to improve hormone levels and ovulation, infant outcomes tend to be better if ovulation occurs spontaneously.

Lack of body fat and excessive body fat around the waist in men is related to decreased production of testosterone and poor sperm quality. Weight gain in underweight men and weight loss in obese men improve testosterone levels and fertility.

As a general rule, individuals who have a body mass index (BMI) of less than 20 or greater than 30 kg/m² are too lean or too fat for optimal fertility. You can determine your BMI by referring to Table 1.1.

BMI isn't always a good indicator of how lean or fat a person is. Individuals who exercise a lot may have a normal BMI but may actually be too lean due to a low percentage of body fat. On the other

TABLE 1.1   DETERMINING YOUR BODY MASS INDEX

BMI	19	20	21	22	23	24	25	26	27	28	29	30	31	32	33	34	35
Height							Weight (lb.)										
4'10" (58")	91	96	100	105	110	115	119	124	129	134	138	143	148	153	158	162	167
4'11" (59")	94	99	104	109	114	119	124	128	133	138	143	148	153	158	163	168	173
5' (60")	97	102	107	112	118	123	128	133	138	143	148	153	158	163	168	174	179
5'1" (61")	100	106	111	116	122	127	132	137	143	148	153	158	164	169	174	180	185
5'2" (62")	104	109	115	120	126	131	136	142	147	153	158	164	169	175	180	186	191
5'3" (63")	107	113	118	124	130	135	141	146	152	158	163	169	175	180	186	191	197
5'4" (64")	110	116	122	128	134	140	145	151	157	163	169	174	180	186	192	197	204
5'5" (65")	114	120	126	132	138	144	150	156	162	168	174	180	186	192	198	204	210
5'6" (66")	118	124	130	136	142	148	155	161	167	173	179	186	192	198	204	210	216
5'7" (67")	121	127	134	140	146	153	159	166	172	178	185	191	198	204	211	217	223
5'8" (68")	125	131	138	144	151	158	164	171	177	184	190	197	203	210	216	223	230
5'9" (69")	128	135	142	149	155	162	169	176	182	189	196	203	209	216	223	230	236
5'10" (70")	132	139	146	153	160	167	174	181	188	195	202	207	216	222	229	236	243
5'11" (71")	136	143	150	157	165	172	179	186	193	200	208	215	222	229	236	243	250
6' (72")	140	147	154	162	169	177	184	191	199	206	213	221	228	235	242	250	258
6'1" (73")	144	151	159	166	174	182	189	197	204	212	219	227	235	242	250	257	265
6'2" (74")	148	155	163	171	179	186	194	202	210	218	225	233	241	249	256	264	272
6'3" (75")	152	160	168	176	184	192	200	208	216	224	232	240	248	256	264	272	279

Source: Evidence Report of Clinical Guidelines on the Identification, Evaluation, and Treatment of Overweight and Obesity in Adults, 1998. NIH/National Heart, Lung, and Blood Institute (NHLBI). cdc.gov.

hand, people who are sedentary may be normal weight but have too much body fat. It is for these individuals that BMI standards may not be a good indicator of body fatness. As a rough guide, a waist circumference over forty-three inches in women and forty-seven inches in men translate into "very high" levels of central body fat.

Tips for Losing Weight and Keeping It Off

If you want to lose weight and keep it off, don't go on fad diets, expect to lose weight rapidly, or rely on diet pills. None of these approaches work in the long run. They are not worth the pain and suffering you have to go through. The most effective way to lose weight and keep it off is to make small changes in your diet and level of exercise. The changes you make should be ones you will find enjoyable and can live with over the long term. Weight loss of one to two pounds a week is a reasonable goal.

Individual food and exercise preferences vary a good deal, so no one diet and exercise plan works for everyone. Individuals need to decide for themselves what and how much they will eat and what types of exercise they would enjoy. The plan should consist of a balanced selection of a variety of basic low-calorie foods. However, you should also include some reduced portions of foods such as sweets, fried foods, and desserts if they'd be missed. You can't make yourself miserable and expect to live with the changes over the long haul.

When you have a plan together that you can happily live with, try it out. Be ready to tweak the plan here and there if parts aren't working. Take time to pat yourself on the back and marvel at your new level of fitness and health. Make it the positive experience and investment in yourself it really is.

Disorders Affecting the Body's Utilization of Nutrients: PCOS and Celiac Disease

A number of conditions that affect the body's utilization of nutrients influence fertility, but two stand out: *PCOS* and *celiac disease.*

PCOS

About 10 percent of women of reproductive age have PCOS, or polycystic ovary syndrome, and it is a leading cause of infertility. It is often underdiagnosed because of variations in signs and symptoms, but women with PCOS generally experience several of the following conditions:

- Irregular menstrual cycles and no ovulation
- Insulin resistance
- Elevated blood levels of androgens (for example, testosterone)
- Polycystic ovaries (the outer layers of the ovaries are thick and hard)
- Central obesity
- Excess body hair
- Elevated blood levels of triglycerides and low levels of HDL cholesterol

Insulin Resistance: A Pivotal Factor for PCOS. The condition is called *insulin resistance* because cells "resist" the action of insulin. One of the functions of insulin is to facilitate the transport of glucose from blood to the inside of cells. With insulin resistance, cells aren't very receptive to the action of insulin, so less glucose enters cells. The body attempts to increase the glucose uptake by cells by producing more insulin. The extra insulin production does help glucose enter cells, but it also causes blood levels of insulin to become abnormally high. High levels of insulin trigger increased production of testosterone by the ovaries, and that disrupts egg development. (Whew.) High testosterone levels lead to excess hair growth on the face and other parts of the body. Abnormally high insulin levels are also related to elevated blood triglyceride and reduced HDL cholesterol levels (HDL cholesterol is the good one; you want high levels.) Women with PCOS are at increased risk of developing infertility, gestational diabetes, hypertension, and heart disease.

The primary goal of treatment for PCOS is decreased insulin resistance and insulin levels. This is best accomplished through weight loss and regular exercise. Reduced levels of insulin kick off a series of beneficial events, including decreased testosterone and triglyceride levels and resumed ovulation. Ergo, fertility returns.

Insulin-sensitizing drugs such as metformin can be used to lower blood testosterone and insulin levels and to stimulate ovulation. Women taking metformin often experience gas and diarrhea as side effects and usually lose weight during the initial months of treatment. It effectively increases the chance of conception. Long term, however, maintaining normal weight and exercise are the keys to managing PCOS and insulin resistance.

Diet, Weight Loss, and PCOS. PCOS is a long-term health concern that requires a sustainable approach to weight loss and exercise. Symptoms of PCOS can improve substantially in women who lose 5 to 10 percent of their initial body weight through diet and exercise. Diets that are most effective for weight loss and insulin reduction in women with PCOS:

- Are calorically reduced
- Are relatively high in protein (15 to 20 percent of calories)
- Are moderate in carbohydrates (45 to 50 percent of calories)
- Emphasize unsaturated fats (such as vegetable oils, fish)

Food sources of carbohydrates should be low GI, meaning those with a low glycemic index (see Table 2.1 in Chapter 2). Low GI carbohydrate foods raise blood glucose and insulin levels less than do high GI foods. Fiber-rich foods, such as whole-grain products, dried beans, fruits, and vegetables, help lower insulin levels and foster weight loss.

Diet and Celiac Disease

As I mentioned earlier, infertility is also associated with untreated celiac disease. Unfortunately, it is often untreated because it isn't identified. *Celiac disease* is a genetically-based condition characterized by a sensitivity to gluten found in wheat, barley, and rye. Ingestion of gluten triggers reactions that damage the lining of the intestines. This damage leads to reduced nutrient absorption, vitamin and mineral deficiencies, diarrhea, constipation, gas, and weight loss. Problems created by gluten sensitivity eventually extend to other body tissues and include bone loss.

It is now recommended that women with infertility from an unknown cause be screened for celiac disease. Untreated celiac disease may lead to a loss of menstrual periods and infertility. In women who become pregnant, it increases the chances of miscarriage and reduced fetal growth. However, there is a highly effective treatment for celiac disease. It's a *gluten-free* diet.

Gluten-free diets lead to a rapid improvement in symptoms in people with newly diagnosed celiac disease. The diet starts with a boom! Many changes need to take place in a short period of time. And the changes have to last a lifetime.

Eliminating gluten from the diet sounds simple enough, but it isn't. Wheat especially is found in some food products where it would be least expected. Did you know sauces, fried foods, and some cultured cheeses contain wheat gluten? Oats, which do not contain gluten, may become contaminated with it during processing. Pasta, breads and bakery products, and many types of cereal contain one or more of the forbidden grains. Fruits, vegetables, nuts, seeds, dry beans, oils, fats, sugars, eggs, milk, and milk products are gluten-free.

People with celiac disease become avid food label readers. As of January 2006, however, it has gotten easier to identify foods with gluten. Products containing wheat now state that fact on the label. Gluten-free food products are becomingly increasingly available at large grocery stores and natural foods markets and from Internet specialty shopping sites. The Additional Resources section at the end of this book lists gluten-free cookbooks and Internet sites where you can join a celiac disease support group or purchase gluten-free products and ingredients. It would also be worthwhile to consult with a registered dietitian experienced in working with people on gluten-free diets, as he or she would have a lot of helpful information to share.

Nutrient Intake

The risk of infertility in women and men is increased by inadequate levels of intake of vitamins C and E, beta-carotene, selenium, vitamin D, and zinc. The risk of infertility may also be increased by low levels of intakes of the omega-3 fatty acids EPA and DHA. Lists of food sources of these nutrients are included in Appendix A, except for EPA and DHA. Food sources of EPA and DHA are listed in Table 4.1 in Chapter 4. Instructions for analyzing the nutrient composition of diets are presented in Chapter 3.

• **Vitamins C and E, beta-carotene, and selenium.** Sperm are rich in polyunsaturated fats, the type found in oils. These fats break down when exposed to oxygen and other reactive chemicals normally present in the body. Antioxidants protect polyunsaturated fats from breaking down and help maintain normal sperm production, structure, and functions. Vitamins C and E, beta-carotene, and selenium protect the polyunsaturated fats in sperm from breakdown due to their action as antioxidants. Several studies have identified improvements in sperm concentration, structure, and motility in men who have corrected deficiencies of these nutrients.

• **Zinc.** Zinc deficiency has long been known to cause infertility in males. A lack of zinc decreases testosterone production and sperm number and motility. Bringing zinc levels up to normal helps restore fertility.

• **Vitamin D.** It appears that a surprisingly high number of women and men in the United States are receiving too little vitamin D from foods and the sun. Poor vitamin D status has many health effects, and the list now includes an effect on fertility. Infertile men with low sperm count are more likely to have low blood levels of vitamin D than men with normal sperm counts.

• **EPA and DHA.** These omega-3 fatty acids participate in egg development and hormone production in women and in sperm development in men. Most U.S. adults who dislike fish or seafood or who eat it infrequently have low intakes. Initial research results suggest that adequate intake of EPA and DHA may help prevent infertility related to hormone production and sperm development.

• **Excess exposure to heavy metals for men.** Men exposed to high levels of lead and mercury may experience infertility due to poor functioning sperm. High blood levels of lead can result from working in smelting and battery factories and from ingesting excess mercury from contaminated fish.

Extremely High Levels of Physical Activity

Exercise-induced or "athletic" menstrual dysfunction is now firmly recognized as a cause of infertility in women. The source of the infertility is usually a loss of periods and ovulation. Women with exercise-induced infertility generally participate in vigorous physical activity for hours a day, have little body fat, and are engaged in intellectual professions with high levels of stress. An eating disorder may also contribute to the loss of menstrual cycles in women with this type of infertility.

Diets of women with exercise-induced infertility are often deficient in calories, vitamins, minerals, and essential fatty acids. Low levels of body fat, nutrient deficiencies, stress, and the wear and tear on the body from vigorous physical activity appear to disrupt secretions of hormones required for fertility. The cure for exercise-induced infertility involves increasing caloric and nutrient intake, decreasing physical activity, and lowering stress.

Excessive Caffeine or Alcohol Consumption

Intakes of over 300 mg caffeine per day, the equivalent of over two cups of brewed coffee, appear to be weakly related to infertility and delayed conception. Coffee intake of two or fewer cups per day appear to be unrelated to fertility. The relationship between caffeine intake and fertility is termed "weak" because some studies show no relationship while other results demonstrate a small effect. One study concluded that high caffeine intake may benefit fertility. It is not clear whether caffeine, something else in coffee, or characteristics of coffee drinkers are responsible for the relationship.

Should you cut back or stop drinking coffee if fertility or delayed conception is a concern? The reasonable response for now is "yes," even though it may or may not help. Regular coffee drinkers should be prepared for "caffeine withdrawal" headaches if they abruptly cut down on coffee. Should you reduce intake of all sources of caffeine or just coffee? The answer to this question depends on whether you are consuming over 300 mg caffeine daily from other sources of caffeine.

Certain teas have a good deal of caffeine and may elevate total caffeine intake to beyond 300 mg daily. Package labels often include

TABLE 1.2   CAFFEINE CONTENT OF BEVERAGES

Beverage	Caffeine (mg)
Coffee, 1 cup	
drip	137–153
percolated	97–125
instant	61–70
decaffeinated	0–4
Tea, 1 cup	
imported	40–176
U.S. brands	32–144
instant iced tea	40–80
Soft drinks, 12 ounces	
Mountain Dew	54
Diet cola	46
Dr. Pepper	40
Coca-Cola	38
Pepsi-Cola	38
Diet Pepsi	37
Ginger ale	0
7-Up	0
Cocoa or chocolate milk, 1 cup	10–17

information on the caffeine content of the tea. In addition, chocolate and many soft drinks contain small amounts of caffeine. Table 1.2 lists the caffeine content of beverages.

Heavy drinking is related to infertility due to the direct, toxic effects of alcohol. Consumption of one or two drinks of alcohol-containing beverages daily does not appear to affect fertility, however. Because alcohol consumption within the first two months after conception may harm the fetus, women are advised to abstain from drinking if they might conceive.

Alternate Approaches to Solving Infertility

Certain herbal remedies, nutrient supplements, and acupuncture may be effective in cases of hormone-related infertility where the cause isn't clear.

Chasteberry (also called *vitex*) may help normalize menstrual cycles. When tested in a product called "Fertility Blend," chasteberry was credited with restoring fertility in 33 percent of infertile women who took it for three months. Fertility Blend also contains green tea extract, arginine, and vitamins and minerals. These components may have had an effect on restoring fertility. Although no harmful side effects were noted, it is too soon to say whether the supplement is completely safe. Chasteberry may have a different effect in men. Legend has it that monks would chew chasteberries to inspire chastity.

Some herbs may interfere with fertility and health, and others are not considered safe for women who may become pregnant. St. John's Wort, echinacea, and ginko, for example, may interfere with conception. Use the Internet resources listed at the back of this book or consult with your health-care provider to investigate the safety and effectiveness of herbs you may consider taking.

Coenzyme Q_{10} is a substance produced by the body that is chemically similar to vitamin E. In one study, coenzyme Q_{10} supplements taken for six months increased sperm motility in men with poor sperm motility of unknown cause. Effects of coenzyme Q_{10} on sperm motility appear to be related to its functions in energy production by sperm and as an antioxidant.

Carnitine, also produced by the body and used in energy production by sperm, appears to increase sperm movement and rates of conception. The study demonstrating this effect gave men L-carnitine and L-acetyl carnitine or a placebo daily for six months. Carnitine appears to be most effective in men with very low levels of sperm motility.

Acupuncture has been tested as a way to increase conception rates in women undergoing *in vitro fertilization* (IVF). One well-designed study showed that women given acupuncture treatments along with IVF were 65 percent more likely to conceive than women not given the treatments. It is speculated that acupuncture increases blood flow to the uterus. Acupuncture costs over $100 per session and may involve two to three sessions per week for several months. These treatments do not improve fertility in women with blocked fallopian tubes or other structural problems that produce infertility.

Studies of the health effects of herbs, nutrients, and other alternative approaches are often limited in scope, small, and short term.

For these reasons, results of these studies are considered preliminary until confirmed by other, well-designed trials. Talk with your health-care provider about alternate treatments you are considering.

Nutrition: One Thing You Can Control

Despite the best efforts, not everyone who wants to become pregnant will, and not all pregnancies will end in healthy newborns. Although it is very important, nutrition is not the only factor that influences fertility or pregnancy. Problems arise due to a myriad of factors that can be identified but not always remedied. In addition, there are probably hundreds of causes of infertility and pregnancy problems that have yet to be identified. These many unknowns make it impossible to chart a course that guarantees conception and a healthy newborn. With so many mysteries, blaming oneself for problems of uncertain origin is unreasonable and should be resisted with all the strength the spirit can muster. Keeping this in mind, the best course to chart is one that is within your control.

One of the best things about nutrition is that the risks associated with poor eating habits can often be eliminated by fixing the diet. It may be as simple as consuming more of your favorite fruits and vegetables, eating a breakfast cereal fortified with folic acid, or taking a low-dose iron supplement. Some steps may be more difficult, such as gaining weight or cutting down on some of your favorite junk foods. But these gifts you give to your unborn baby will benefit you as well. Your reward may be a perfectly timed conception, higher energy levels during pregnancy, less intense side effects, or a fully grown and developed newborn who is easy to care for. The specific information you need to follow the right nutrition path will be provided to you in the upcoming chapters.

$\backsim$ 2 $\backsim$

The Truth About Nutrition and Healthy Diets

"All things in nutriment are good or bad relatively."

—Hippocrates

Welcome to Nutrition 101: A crash course on how substances in foods affect health. Unlike a typical college course, the contents are condensed, and there are no tuition costs, pop quizzes, or papers due. It is included in this book to provide you good, general background information about nutrition and to help you make the right decisions about your diet. Use this chapter to learn as much, or as little, as you want or need, and remember it's here if you need to look up a fact or to check out something you read or hear about nutrition.

In this chapter, you will find information on nutrients and other substances in foods that benefit health, recommended levels of nutrient intake, vegetarianism, and how to obtain a healthy diet. The final section of the chapter provides a prescription for diagnosing the truthfulness of nutrition information presented to consumers.

Ten Nutrition Principles

Without some guidelines, it can be very difficult to determine if what you hear or read about nutrition is fact or fantasy. This chapter presents core knowledge, or principles, upon which the science of nutrition is based. Included within the discussion are ways this knowledge can be personally applied to promote health before, during, and after pregnancy. Subsequent chapters address the application of nutrition knowledge to fertility, pregnancy, infant feeding, and breast-feeding. The basic truths about nutrition can be summarized in ten principles. These principles change little with time and serve as the foundation for growth in knowledge about nutrition and health.

1. Food Is a Basic Need of Humans

The first nutrition principle is straightforward. Humans need food to grow, to reproduce, and to stay healthy. Food also represents one of the greatest pleasures on Earth. It provides relief from hunger and a feeling of comfort and security. Beyond survival, food is basic to a full and healthy life.

2. Food Provides Sustenance Needed for Growth and Health

The human body requires nutrients, or specific chemical substances in food that perform particular functions in the body. There are only six categories of nutrients:

- Carbohydrates
- Proteins
- Fats
- Vitamins
- Minerals
- Water

Carbohydrates, proteins, and fats supply calories and are called the *energy nutrients*. Although these three types of nutrients perform a variety of functions, they share the property of being the body's source of energy. Vitamins, minerals, and water are primarily needed for the conversion of carbohydrates, proteins, and fats into energy and for the building and maintenance of muscles, blood components, bones, and other body parts. Water serves as a medium for most chemical reactions that take place in the body; it is needed for the removal of waste products in urine; and it functions as the body's cooling system.

The Energy Nutrients

The first and foremost need of the body is for energy, or the *calories* supplied by food. Calories are not a component of food. Rather, they represent the amount of energy supplied by the carbohydrate, protein, and fat content of foods. Most carbohydrates and proteins supply four calories per gram, while fat provides over twice that much—nine calories per gram. (There are twenty-eight grams in one ounce; one ounce is two tablespoons of liquid.) If you have observed the flames produced by dripping fat from a steak or hamburger on a grill, you have seen the powerhouse of energy stored in fat. Foods high in carbohydrates or protein, such as corn, potatoes, fish, or shrimp, don't burn with nearly the same intensity when grilled. They have less energy to give. Alcohol, a fermentation product of carbohydrates, provides seven calories per gram. The relatively high energy content of alcohol makes the preparation of cherries jubilee and crepes suzette possible.

When we consume more calories from food than our bodies need, the excess is largely converted to fat and stored for later use. The body is not picky. It converts excessive incoming supplies of carbohydrates, fats, and proteins into storage fat. Carbohydrates can also be stored in the body in the form of glycogen. However, glycogen stores are much smaller than our fat stores. People are usually limited to about an eighteen-hundred-calorie supply of glycogen stored in muscles and the liver. The human ability to store fat, on the other hand, can be extraordinary and averages about one hundred forty thousand calories in adults. When fewer calories are taken in than needed, we draw upon our energy stores, reducing both them and our overall weight.

There is much more to learn about the energy nutrients. This information is condensed into the highlights that follow.

Carbohydrates

Carbohydrates are the world's leading source of human energy. Foods rich in carbohydrates, such as rice, potatoes, dried beans, millet, cassava, pasta, and breads, are the main ingredients of people's diets throughout most of the world. The United States and several other economically developed countries stand out from the rest of the world in that carbohydrates take a back seat to foods rich in protein and fat. Many different substances in foods are classified as carbohydrates. The two major types are *simple sugars* and *complex carbohydrates*. Alcohol, because it is formed from carbohydrates, is categorized as a carbohydrate-like substance.

Carbohydrates are now classified by their *glycemic index*. Carbohydrate-containing foods (such as potatoes, tortilla, and peas) have a range of effects on blood glucose levels. Some cause a large increase in blood glucose levels and others do not. Foods that increase blood glucose to relatively high levels require more insulin to move glucose into cells than do foods that produce lower levels of glucose. The glycemic index (GI) of a carbohydrate-containing food is based on how much it increases blood glucose level. Foods with a low GI produce lower blood glucose levels and insulin requirements compared to foods with moderate or high GI values.

It is tempting to categorize sugary and very sweet foods as high GI foods and "starchy" foods like potatoes and rice as low GI. That's not the way it works. To know the GI value of foods, you have to look the food up in a table (see Table 2.1). GI values are being increasingly used to guide carbohydrate-containing food selection by people with diabetes, insulin resistance, and other conditions related to blood insulin levels.

Simple Sugars. There are three major sugars that are as simple as carbohydrates get: glucose (blood sugar), fructose (fruit sugar), and galactose (milk sugar). Nearly all of the fructose and galactose consumed in foods is rapidly converted to glucose by the body. Glucose

TABLE 2.1   GLYCEMIC INDEX (GI) OF SOME
CARBOHYDRATE-RICH FOODS

High GI (>70)	Medium GI (50–70)	Low GI (<50)
Beverages		
Gatorade	Cola	Apple juice
Lucozade	Cranberry juice cocktail	Carrot juice
Orange juice	Grapefruit juice	
Orange soda	Pineapple juice	
Sustagen Sport		
Tomato juice		
Breads and Cereals		
Bagel, whole wheat	Bran Buds	All Bran
Bran flakes	Bread, cracked wheat	Barley
Bread, French	Chapati	Bread, rye
Bread, wheat	Couscous	Cassava
Bread, white	Cream of Wheat	Muesli
Cheerios	Croissants	Oat bran
Coco Puffs	Just Right	Pasta
Corn Chex	Life	Tortilla, corn/wheat
Cornflakes	Muffin, blueberry	
Corn Pops	Oatmeal	
Doughnut, cake	Pancakes	
Grapenuts	Pita bread	
Popcorn	Rice, white/brown	
Puffed Wheat	Raisin Bran	
Pretzels		
Rice Krispies		
Shredded Wheat		
Soda crackers		
Total		
Waffles		
Fruits and Vegetables		
French fries	Banana	Apple
Potato, baked	Corn	Beans, dry
Potato, instant mashed	Mango	Cherries
Watermelon	Potato, boiled	Grapefruit
Sweet potato	Grapes	
Hummus		
Kiwi		
Orange		

continued

**TABLE 2.1   GLYCEMIC INDEX (GI) OF SOME
CARBOHYDRATE-RICH FOODS,** *continued*

High GI (>70)	Medium GI (50–70)	Low GI (<50)
Fruits and Vegetables, *continued*		
Peach		
Pear		
Peas, green		
Plums		
Yams		
Sweets and Candy		
Fruit Roll-up	Honey	Fructose
Glucose	Mars Bar	Lactose
Jelly beans	Power Bar	M&M's, peanut
Table sugar	Milk chocolate	
Snickers		
Twix		
Xylitol		

is the only form of sugar that can be used by the body to make energy.

Simple sugars come in packages of two units of glucose, fructose, and/or galactose. Maltose (malt sugar) consists of two units of glucose, whereas sucrose (table sugar) and honey are formed from glucose and fructose. The milk sugar lactose contains glucose plus galactose.

Most of the simple sugars have a very distinctive sweet taste, which is why many people love to eat them. Humans, like most mammals, are born with a preference for sweet-tasting foods. Even before birth, a fetus will move toward a sucrose solution injected into the womb and will withdraw from bitter and sour-tasting fluids. After birth, infants will select sweet-tasting liquids over those with other flavors. Interestingly, breast milk tastes sweet.

Most of the simple sugars in the American diet are added to foods before purchase. Of the total amount of sugar produced, about 65 percent is used by the food and beverage industry and the manufacturers of soft drinks, beer, wine, bakery products, cereals, candy, and processed foods. One twelve-ounce cola, for example, contains about eight teaspoons of sugar. Some presweetened cereals have four teaspoons of added sugar per serving. Added sugars can make up as much as 45 percent of the total calories in breakfast cereal. You can find out how much sugar is in a breakfast cereal, or in many other foods, by checking the nutrition information panel on the package.

Is there good reason to swallow a side order of guilt along with your favorite treats? Do sweets deserve their reputation as being bad for you? Do they cause hyperactivity, diabetes, obesity, and tooth decay?

Sugars, by themselves, are not bad for you, nor are they responsible for hyperactivity in children, diabetes, or obesity. It is true that frequent snacking on sweet foods and a failure to clean your teeth after consuming sticky sweets can lead to tooth decay. This is much more likely to occur in people whose local water supply is not fluoridated.

There is another problem related to sugars that depends on the quantity of sugary foods consumed. Goodies like candy, sherbet, soft drinks, and cookies are usually a poor source of vitamins, minerals, and other beneficial components of food. If too many sweet foods are eaten, they replace other, more nutrient-dense foods in the diet, such as vegetables, fruits, and whole-grain products. Large intakes of sweet foods can contribute to weight gain and from there to disorders such as Type 2 diabetes, hypertension, and heart disease.

Complex Carbohydrates. Complex carbohydrates consist of starches, glycogen, and dietary fiber (or *bulk*). Complex carbohydrates come to us from plants and, although many are formed by combinations of glucose units, they all lack the sweet taste of simple sugars. Because animal products contain very little glycogen, almost all of the starch in our diets comes from plant sources, such as dried beans, potatoes, corn, wheat, and rice. These plants store glucose as starch. Starch consumed in the diet is broken down by digestive enzymes into glucose. Food sources of starch are not only high in glucose, but they provide vitamins, minerals, dietary fiber, and other elements required for health.

Recommendations for health-promoting diets indicate that 45 to 65 percent of our total calories should come from carbohydrates, particularly food sources of the complex carbohydrates (see Table 2.2).

TABLE 2.2   FOOD SOURCES OF COMPLEX CARBOHYDRATES

	Amount	Complex Carbohydrates (grams)	Percent of Total Calories from Complex Carbohydrates
Grain and Grain Products			
Rice	½ cup	21	83
Pasta	½ cup	15	81
Cornflakes	1 cup	11	76
Oatmeal	1½ cups	12	74
Cheerios	1 cup	11	68
Whole-wheat bread	1 slice	7	60
Dried Beans (cooked)			
Lima beans	½ cup	11	64
White beans	½ cup	13	63
Kidney beans	½ cup	12	59
Vegetables			
Carrot	1 medium	7	93
Potato	1 medium	30	85
Corn	½ cup	10	67
Broccoli	½ cup	2	40

Fiber. Fiber differs from starches in that it is not digested by enzymes produced by humans. It is a caloric bargain. Since we don't digest fiber, it is not considered a source of calories. Plant foods such as fruits, vegetables, whole-grain products, seeds, and dry beans provide fiber. Even though we don't digest it, fiber plays important roles in the body. Fiber provides a sense of fullness, reduces post-meal increases in blood glucose level, prevents constipation, and decreases cholesterol absorption.

Many foods, such as dried beans, potatoes, and avocados, hide their high fiber content very well. They are not crunchy and don't look fibrous. Yet they are among our best sources of dietary fiber. Other foods that are crunchy, such as popcorn, lettuce, and celery, are not very high in fiber. The bottom line is that you can't tell a food's fiber content by its looks or its crunch value. Table 2.3 shows the dietary fiber content of many foods and reveals the hidden truths.

TABLE 2.3   FOOD SOURCES OF FIBER

	Amount	Dietary Fiber (grams)
Grain and Cereal Products		
Bran Buds	1 cup	24
Bulgur, cooked	1 cup	11
All Bran	½ cup	10
40% Bran Flakes	1 cup	8
Bran muffin	1 large (4 ounces)	7
Cornmeal muffin	1 large (4 ounces)	7
Bran Chex	1 cup	7
Raisin Bran	1 cup	7
Bran	¼ cup	6
Grape-Nuts	¾ cup	6
Whole-wheat macaroni	1 cup	5
Shredded Wheat	1 biscuit	3
Oatmeal	¾ cup	2
Cornflakes	¾ cup	2
Whole-wheat bread	1 slice	2
Popcorn	2 cups	2
Fruits		
Avocado, mashed	1 cup	7
Raspberries	1 cup	5
Mango	1 medium	4
Pear (with skin)	1 medium	4
Strawberries	1 cup	4
Apple (with skin)	1 medium	3
Peach (with skin)	1 medium	3
Banana or plantain	6 inches long	2
Vegetables		
Corn, canned	½ cup	5
Lima beans	½ cup	5
Potato (with skin)	1 medium	3
Potato (no skin)	1 medium	2
Broccoli	½ cup	3
Carrots, boiled	½ cup	3
Green beans	½ cup	3
Brussels sprouts	½ cup	3
Eggplant	½ cup	3
Collard greens	½ cup	3

continued

TABLE 2.3   FOOD SOURCES OF FIBER, *continued*

	Amount	Dietary Fiber (grams)
Nuts		
Almonds, Brazil nuts	1 ounce	3
Peanuts, pecans, macadamias	1 ounce	2
Peanut butter	2 tablespoons	2
Dried Beans		
Pinto beans	½ cup	10
Black beans	½ cup	8
White, kidney, navy beans	½ cup	7
Garbanzos (chickpeas)	½ cup	5
Lentils	½ cup	5
Peas	½ cup	4

Many people consume too little dietary fiber. Approximately twenty-five grams per day for women and thirty-eight grams daily for men represent healthful levels of intake. Individuals vary in their ability to tolerate increased levels of dietary fiber. If you develop diarrhea after increasing your fiber intake, cut back. Remember to increase your fluid intake if you add fiber to your diet to avoid constipation.

Although human beings do not produce the types of digestive enzymes needed to break down dietary fiber, certain bacteria that dwell in the large intestines do. Bacteria that consume dietary fiber as food don't break down the fiber completely. They excrete fragments of fats and gases as end products of dietary fiber ingestion. Discomfort related to bacterial gas production with dietary fiber intake decreases over time.

Protein

There is little reason to write about the importance of protein; most people are already convinced of it. Protein is an essential structural component of all living matter. It is involved in most every biological process that takes place in humans. Although protein is used as an energy source, this is a secondary, rather than primary, role.

Proteins consist of units of amino acids linked together in chemical chains. It is really the amino acids that are needed for health, not the protein per se. There are twenty amino acids that serve as building blocks for the thousands of proteins formed by the body. Of these, nine are *essential*, meaning that they must be obtained through diet. The other eleven major amino acids are considered *nonessential* because they can be produced by the body. They still perform necessary roles in the body, however, and they are as important to health as the essential amino acids. They are only called *nonessential* because we don't have to obtain them from foods.

Proteins are classified by their ability to support protein tissue construction in the body. Not all sources of protein do this equally well; it depends on the essential amino acids they contain. How well proteins in foods support the development and maintenance of protein tissues in the body is discovered by tests of the protein's *quality*.

Protein Quality. Proteins are different from carbohydrates and fats in that they vary in quality. In general, animal products provide high-quality protein, and plant foods have lower protein quality. Unless proteins of high quality are eaten, people will not grow, reproduce, or stay healthy, no matter how much protein is consumed.

High-quality proteins contain all of the essential amino acids in the amounts needed to support protein tissue formation in the body. If any of the essential amino acids are lacking in dietary protein sources, protein tissues are not formed—even for those proteins that could be constructed from available amino acids. It may appear inefficient for the body to shut off protein tissue construction for the want of an amino acid or two. If protein tissue development did not shut down, however, cells would end up with an imbalanced assortment of protein that would seriously affect cell functions. Without the needed levels of each essential amino acid, proteins consumed can only be used to form energy.

Food sources of protein that contain all of the essential amino acids in the amounts needed to support protein tissue construction are considered high quality, or *complete proteins*. Proteins in this category include those found in animal products, such as meat, milk, and eggs. *Incomplete proteins* are deficient in one or more amino acids. With the exception of soybean protein for adults, proteins found in plants are incomplete. However, you can complement the essential amino acids composition of plant sources by combining them to form a complete source of protein. Combining a grain such as rice with a legume such as pinto beans provides a complete protein source. Complementary proteins can be obtained from plants by combining rice and green peas, bulgur and dried beans, barley and dried beans, corn and dried beans, corn and lima beans, and seeds and green peas. Although it used to be thought that complementary proteins needed to be consumed at the same meal, this is no longer considered to be true.

Excessively restrictive or poorly planned vegetarian diets, especially when consumed by people with high nutrient needs, such as children and pregnant women, can compromise health. Well-planned vegetarian diets, however, are nutrient dense and health promoting.

Adult women and men require about fifty grams of protein a day, and most American adults consume far more protein than that. It is recommended that adults consume somewhere between 10 to 35 percent of their total calories from protein. You can estimate whether you are getting the right amount by examining Table 2.4.

Fats

Fats are a group of substances found in the body that have one major property in common: They dissolve in fat and not in water. If you have ever tried to get vinegar and oil to mix before you poured them over a salad, you have observed firsthand the principle of water and fat solubility.

Fats are actually a subcategory of the fat-soluble substances known as *lipids*. Lipids include all types of fats and oils. Fats are often distinguished from oils by their property of being solid at room temperature. Solid fat is generally high in saturated fat and of animal origin. Butter, lard, and animal fat belong in this group because they don't melt at room temperature. Oils, on the other hand, are liquid at room temperature. They contain primarily unsaturated fats from plants. A liquid oil can be changed to a solid fat by adding hydrogens, called *hydrogenating* the oil. Hydrogenated fats, such as margarine and shortening, still contain an abundance of unsaturated fats.

TABLE 2.4   FOOD SOURCES OF PROTEIN

Food	Amount	Grams	Percent of Total Calories
Animal Products			
Beef steak, lean	3 ounces	26	60
Chicken, baked, no skin	3 ounces	24	60
Hamburger, lean	3 ounces	24	34
Tuna in water	3 ounces	24	89
Beef roast, lean	3 ounces	23	45
Salmon, broiled	3 ounces	23	50
Pork chop, lean	3 ounces	20	59
Fish (haddock)	3 ounces	19	4
Cottage cheese, low-fat	½ cup	14	69
Yogurt, low-fat	1 cup	13	34
Shrimp	3 ounces	11	84
Milk, skim	1 cup	9	40
Milk, whole	1 cup	8	23
Milk, 2% fat	1 cup	8	26
Swiss cheese	1 ounce	8	30
Cheddar cheese	1 ounce	7	25
Egg	1 medium	6	32
Dried Beans and Nuts			
Tofu	½ cup	14	38
Soybeans, cooked	½ cup	10	33
Peanuts	¼ cup	9	17
Black or navy beans, cooked	½ cup	8	26
Peanut butter	2 tablespoons	8	17
Walnuts	¼ cup	8	14
Almonds	¼ cup	7	13
Lima beans, cooked	½ cup	6	27
Split peas, cooked	½ cup	5	31
Grains			
Noodles, cooked	1 cup	7	25
Corn	1 cup	5	29
Oatmeal, cooked	1 cup	5	15
Macaroni, cooked	1 cup	5	13
White rice, cooked	1 cup	4	11
Brown rice, cooked	1 cup	4	10
Whole-wheat bread	1 slice	2	15
White bread	1 slice	2	13

The hydrogenation process converts some unsaturated fats into trans fats. These types of fat contribute to clogged arteries. Improved processing techniques and new requirements for labeling the trans fat content of packaged foods are leading to substantially reduced levels of these harmful fats in processed foods.

Fats in foods supply not only energy, but also fat-soluble nutrients. Fats carry essential fatty acids and the fat-soluble vitamins A, D, E, and K. So part of the reason that we need fats in our diets is to get a supply of the essential nutrients they carry. Fats are important to our taste buds in that fat increases the flavor of food. Fat in our body cushions organs, helps maintain a normal body temperature, and serves as a structural component of all cell membranes and nerves.

Recommendations for fat intake have changed substantially over recent years. Rather than recommend that people consume a certain amount of fat, new recommendations focus on type of fat. Fats considered healthful are *unsaturated*, and two omega-3 fatty acids, *EPA* (eicosapentaenoic acid) and *DHA* (docosahexaenoic acid) now qualify for the healthful fats list. These two fatty acids help prevent heart disease, reduce blood pressure and triglyceride levels, decrease insulin resistance, improve cognition, and enhance fetal and infant development. People now want to focus on unhealthful fats, which include *saturated* and trans fats as well as foods high in cholesterol.

High fat intake is related to excessive caloric intake, obesity, certain types of cancer, and diabetes. Diets high in saturated fats promote heart disease, especially in men. Nutrition information labels on food packages identify grams of fat in a serving of food and the percent of calories from fat. Also listed on nutrition information labels are grams of saturated fat, monounsaturated fat, polyunsaturated fat, trans fat, and cholesterol in a serving. Refer to Table 2.5 to identify the fat content of common foods.

Cholesterol. Cholesterol is a close chemical relative of fat. It is a clear, oily liquid that is distributed in both the fatty and lean portions of many animal products. It is also produced by the human liver. Cholesterol is used by the body to form hormones and vitamin D and is a component of all cell membranes. Beef, poultry, and seafood provide 30 to 80 mg of cholesterol per three-ounce serv-

TABLE 2.5   FOOD SOURCES OF FAT

Food	Amount	Fat Content Grams	Percent of Total Calories
Fats and Oils			
Gravy	¼ cup	14	77
Mayonnaise	1 tablespoon	11	99
Heavy cream	1 tablespoon	6	93
Salad dressing	1 tablespoon	6	83
Oil	1 teaspoon	5	100
Butter	1 teaspoon	4	100
Margarine	1 teaspoon	4	100
Meats, Eggs			
Whopper	8.9 ounces	32	48
Big Mac	6.6 ounces	31	52
Quarter Pounder with cheese	6.8 ounces	29	50
Pork or beef with fat	3 ounces	18	62
Sausage	4 links	18	77
Hamburger, regular (20% fat)	3 ounces	17	62
Hot dog	1 (2 ounces)	17	83
Chicken, fried with skin	3 ounces	14	53
Salmon	3 ounces	11	46
Salami	2 ounces	11	68
Hamburger, lean (10% fat)	3 ounces	10	45
Steak (rib eye)	3 ounces	10	47
Steak (T-bone, lean)	3 ounces	9	44
Bacon	3 pieces	9	74
Bologna	1 ounce	8	80
Tuna in oil, drained	3 ounces	7	38
Egg	1	6	68
Steak (round, lean only)	3 ounces	5	29
Chicken, baked, without skin	3 ounces	4	25
Venison	3 ounces	3	14
Hamburger, extra lean (4% fat)	3 ounces	2	23
Flounder, baked	3 ounces	1	13
Shrimp, boiled	3 ounces	1	7
Haddock	3 ounces	1	7

continued

TABLE 2.5   FOOD SOURCES OF FAT, *continued*

		Fat Content	
Food	Amount	Grams	Percent of Total Calories
Milk and Milk Products			
Cheddar cheese	1 ounce	9.5	74
Milk, whole	1 cup	8.5	49
American cheese	1 ounce	6	66
Cottage cheese, regular	½ cup	5.1	39
Milk, 2% fat	1 cup	5	32
Milk, 1% fat	1 cup	2.7	24
Cottage cheese, 1% fat	½ cup	1.2	13
Milk, skim	1 cup	0.4	4
Other			
French fries	20 fries	20	49
Walnuts	1 ounce	17.6	87
Peanuts	¼ cup	17.5	75
Veggie Pita	1	17	38
Sunflower seeds	¼ cup	17	77
Avocado	½	15	84
Almonds	1 ounce	15	80
Cashews	1 ounce	13.2	73
Potato chips	1 ounce (13 chips)	11	61
Chocolate chip cookies	4	11	54
Peanut butter	1 tablespoon	8	76
Taco chips	1 ounce (10 chips)	6.2	41
Mashed potatoes	½ cup	4.5	41
Olives	4 medium	1.5	90
Baked potato	1	0.2	1
Candy			
Mr. Goodbar	1.7 ounces	15	56
Peanut butter cups, 2 regular	1.6 ounces	15	54
Milk chocolate	1.6 ounces	14	53
Almond Joy	1.8 ounces	14	50
Twix	2 ounces	14	45
Baby Ruth	2.1 ounces	14	43
M & M's, peanut	1.7 ounces	13	47
Kit Kat	1.5 ounces	12	47
Snickers	2.1 ounces	13	42
PayDay	1.9 ounces	12	43

TABLE 2.5 FOOD SOURCES OF FAT, *continued*

		Fat Content	
Food	Amount	Grams	Percent of Total Calories
Rolo, 10 candies	1.9 ounces	12	40
Butterfinger	2.1 ounces	12	39
Sno-Caps	2.3 ounces	12	34
Nestle's Crunch	1.6 ounces	11	45
Milky Way	2.2 ounces	11	35
M & M's, plain	1.7 ounces	10	39
Whoppers	1.8 ounces	10	38
Three Musketeers	2.1 ounces	9	31
Raisinets	1.6 ounces	8	38
Milky Way II	2.2 ounces	5.5	26

ing, whereas dairy products provide less than 30 mg per serving. Liver and eggs are the two richest sources of cholesterol in our diets. Cholesterol is not "fattening." It is not used by the body as a source of energy.

People are urged to consume less than 300 mg of cholesterol daily and most women do consume less than that amount. Actually, cholesterol intake is much more weakly associated with heart disease than is saturated or trans fat intake. In addition, it is not clear whether high saturated fat and high cholesterol intake increase the risk of heart disease in most women.

Vitamins and Minerals

Humans require the thirteen vitamins and fifteen minerals listed in Table 2.6. If you see other substances labeled as vitamins or other minerals labeled as "essential," they are bogus. This rule applies, by the way, to lecithin, enzymes, coenzymes, and other substances sold as essential for health but that the body produces.

Compared to the energy nutrients, vitamins and minerals are required in small amounts by the body. Vitamins facilitate the formation of energy in body tissues and help protect the body from various diseases. Minerals serve as structural components of body

TABLE 2.6 VITAMINS AND MINERALS REQUIRED BY HUMANS

Vitamins	Minerals
The B-complex vitamins	Calcium
Thiamin (B_1)	Chloride
Riboflavin (B_2)	Chromium
Niacin (B_3)	Copper
B_6 (pyridoxine)	Fluoride
Folate (folacin, folic acid)	Iodine
B_{12} (cyanocobalamin)	Iron
Biotin	Magnesium
Pantothenic acid (pantothenate)	Manganese
Vitamin C (ascorbic acid)	Potassium
Vitamin A (retinol)	Molydbenum
Vitamin D (1,25 dihidroxy-colicalciferol)	Phosphorus
Vitamin E (tocopherol)	Selenium
Vitamin K (phylloquinone, menadione)	Sodium
	Zinc

tissues and are needed for the regulation of energy formation, nervous system function, and water balance.

Four of the vitamins are fat soluble (vitamins D, E, K, and A, or "Deka"), while the other nine vitamins are water soluble. Because fat-soluble vitamins are stored in fat tissues, we generally have enough of these vitamins to last several months when dietary intake becomes low. With the exception of vitamin B_{12}, which can be stored in amounts that last for several years, the water-soluble vitamins are not stored in large amounts. Inadequate levels of intake of the water-soluble vitamins produce deficiency symptoms within a few weeks to a few months after dietary supply has stopped. If we fail to consume enough of each vitamin and essential mineral in our diets, specific deficiency diseases develop. On the other hand, if we consume excessive amounts of vitamins and minerals, overdose reactions occur.

The diverse functions of vitamins and minerals, as well as consequences of deficiency and overdose, major food sources, and other facts about vitamins and minerals are listed in Appendix A.

Preserving the Vitamin and Mineral Content of Foods. Major losses of vitamins and minerals may occur during food storage and preparation. Overcooking, holding cooked foods on a warmer or steam table, and cooking foods in lots of water and tossing out the water that the foods are cooked in all result in vitamin and mineral losses. (Overcooking vegetables should be a nutritional misdemeanor. In addition to causing vitamin and mineral losses, it tends to make people dislike vegetables!) Green beans and peas, if held hot for three hours before served, lose over half their content of thiamin, riboflavin, and vitamin C. Approximately one third of the vitamin content of boiled vegetables is tossed out with the cooking water. The following lists give tips for preserving the vitamin and mineral content of foods.

Storing Foods

- Store foods for the shortest amount of time possible.
- Choose fresh, freeze-dried, and frozen products over heavily processed products.
- Store vegetables and fruits not needing refrigeration in a cool, dry, and clean place.
- Store leftover, perishable foods tightly wrapped in a refrigerator that is set just above 32°F.
- Avoid the freeze-thaw-freeze cycle. Foods defrosted, heated, and then refrozen show major losses in vitamin content.

Preparing Foods

- Don't overcook foods, especially vegetables. Cook most vegetables to the point where they are still a bit crunchy.
- Microwave, stir-fry, steam, or broil foods. Use just enough water to prevent scorching.
- Serve foods right after they have been prepared (or be the first one in the cafeteria line). Time food preparation so that the foods served are all ready at the same time.

Antioxidant Nutrients. Beta-carotene (a precursor of vitamin A), vitamins E and C, and selenium (an essential mineral) function as *antioxidants*. A variety of plant pigments and a number of enzymes produced by the body also function as antioxidants. These substances prevent or repair damage to cells caused by exposure to oxygen, ozone, smoke, and other oxidizing agents. Lack of sufficient levels of antioxidants in body tissues is related to premature aging, some types of cancer, inflammation, bronchitis, emphysema, heart disease, cataracts, and pregnancy complications. People who consume five or more servings of fruits and vegetables each day tend to have better levels of intake of antioxidants than people who eat them less often.

Other Important Components of Food

There is a wide variety of substances in food that are not required in our diets yet perform important functions in the body. We are just beginning to discover the beneficial health effects of compounds such as flavinols in dark grapes and red wine; plant pigments such as anthocyanins (red-purple), lycopene (red), luetin (yellow-green); and isoflavones in soy products. When regularly consumed, these "phytochemicals" appear to provide protection against a host of disorders, including certain infectious diseases, cataracts, heart disease, and some types of cancer. It is too soon to know how much of them is best to consume. The recommendation that adults consume two cups of fruits and two to three cups of vegetables daily is based, in part, on the health benefits of these nonnutrient components of plant foods.

It should be noted that plant foods are superior to phytochemical extracts or pills for delivering these benefits. Phytochemicals in plants appear to work together with nutrients in foods to favorably affect health.

Recommended Levels of Nutrient Intake

The Dietary Reference Intakes (DRIs) are the most widely used standard for identifying desired levels of nutrient intake (see Table 2.7). DRIs values are age, sex, and condition (pregnant or lactating) specific.

Nutrient amounts set in the DRI tables on Recommended Dietary Intakes for individuals are sufficient to meet the needs of 98 percent of healthy people throughout their lifecycle. A margin of safety is built into the values, so intakes that approximate the rec-

TABLE 2.7 DIETARY REFERENCE INTAKES FOR PREGNANT AND BREAST-FEEDING WOMEN

	Women	Pregnancy	Lactation
Energy, calories	2,403	13–26 wks: +340 26–40 wks: +452	0–6 mo: +330 6–12 mo: +400
Protein, grams	46	71	71
Fiber, grams	25	28	29
Water, cups	11	12.5	16
Vitamins			
A, mcg	700 (2,330 IU)	770 (2,564 IU)	1,300 (4,329 IU)
C, mg	75	85	120
D, mcg	5 (200 IU)	5 (200 IU)	5 (200 IU)
E, mg	15 (22 IU)	15 (22 IU)	19 (28 IU)
K, mcg	90	90	90
Thiamin (B_1), mg	1.1	1.4	1.4
Riboflavin (B_2), mg	1.1	1.4	1.6
Niacin (B_3), mg	14	18	17
B_6, mg	1.3	1.9	2
Folate, mcg	400	600	500
B_{12}, mcg	2.4	2.6	2.8
Pantothenic acid, mg	5	6	7
Biotin, mcg	30	30	35
Minerals			
Calcium, mg	1,000	1,000	1,000
Chromium, mcg	25	30	45
Copper, mcg	900	1,000	1,300
Fluoride, mg	3	3	3
Iodine, mcg	150	220	290
Iron, mg	18	27	9
Magnesium, mg	310	350	310
Manganese, mg	1.8	2	2.6
Molybdenum, mcg	45	50	50
Phosphorus, mg	700	700	700
Selenium, mcg	55	60	70
Zinc, mg	8	11	12
Sodium, g	1.5	1.5	1.5
Chloride, g	2.3	2.3	2.3
Potassium, g	4.7	4.7	5.1

Recommended intake levels represent Recommended Dietary Allowance (RDA) and Adequate Intake (AI) levels for women 19 to 30 years old. Note: mcg = micrograms (also abbreviated ug), mg = milligrams, and g = grams.

Source: Data from the Dietary Reference Intake (DRI) Reports 1997–2002, published by the National Academy of Sciences. You can obtain the DRI tables covering nutrient needs for people of all ages from nal.usda.gov/fnic/etext/000105.html.

ommended levels are likely sufficient. The DRI Tables also list "Tolerable Upper Intake Levels," or levels of nutrient intake that can cause harm if exceeded. (Additional information on the DRIs can be found on the Internet by searching for the term "Dietary Reference Intakes.")

3. Health Problems Related to Nutrition Originate Within Cells

All body processes required for growth and health take place within cells and the fluid that surrounds them. There are over one hundred trillion cells in the body to help with these processes. Functions of cells are maintained by the nutrients they receive. Health problems can arise when a cell's need for nutrients differs from the available supply. An excess supply of vitamin A in cells during growth, for example, can cause abnormal bone formation, and too little calcium and vitamin D at any time during life decrease bone density. You are as healthy as your cells.

4. Poor Nutrition Can Result from Both Inadequate and Excessive Levels of Nutrient Intake

The main point of this principle is that you can become malnourished by consuming too little or too much of the nutrients. For each nutrient, there is a range of intake that is compatible with optimal functioning of the nutrient in the body. Up to a point, the body can adapt to low or high intakes of nutrients by using nutrient stores or by excreting excessive levels of nutrients through the urine or stools. Nutrient-deficiency diseases or overdose symptoms result when we exceed the body's capacity to adjust for low or high levels of intake. If we consume too little vitamin C, for example, the body calls upon its limited store of vitamin C; when this runs out, signs of a deficiency begin to develop. Deficiency symptoms may start within as little as a month without vitamin C intake. The first sign of a deficiency is usually delayed wound healing. If allowed to progress, the vitamin C deficiency leads to gums that bleed easily, pain and bruising upon being touched, and abnormal bone growth. Excessive intake of vitamin C (a gram or more daily) produces diarrhea and may contribute to the development of kidney stones. Nearly all cases of vitamin or mineral overdose result from the excessive use of supplements.

5. Humans Have Adaptive Mechanisms for Managing Fluctuations in Nutrient Intake

To a certain extent, the body can cope with low and high levels of nutrient availability. It can decrease absorption of some nutrients when intake levels or body stores are high, excrete excess in stools or urine, and store needed nutrients in various tissues and organs. These built-in mechanisms provide an important buffer against deficiency and toxicity diseases and other health problems. But they do not protect humans from all of the consequences of poor nutrition.

6. Malnutrition Results from Poor Diets and Conditions, Disease, Genetic Factors, or Combinations of These Causes

People can become malnourished by way of inadequate or excessive levels of nutrient intake or because body functions are impaired due to genetic predisposition, surgery, poor health, or certain medications. Bleeding ulcers, for example, are a common cause of iron deficiency in the elderly. People who have a condition that causes the storage of too much iron suffer from iron overdose. Impairments in bodily functions in people with cancer and HIV/AIDS frequently lead to malnutrition.

7. Some People Are at Higher Risk of Becoming Inadequately Nourished Than Others

The risk of poor nutrition is not shared equally among all people. Individuals with a high need for nutrients due to pregnancy, breastfeeding, growth, illness, or recovery from illness or surgery will develop malnutrition faster in times of food shortage than will healthy people. In cases of widespread famine, such as that induced by natural disasters or war, the health of nutritionally vulnerable groups is compromised soonest and most. The younger the person at the time of a food shortage, and the longer the shortage of food exists, the more lasting are the ill effects on health and mental development.

8. Poor Nutrition Can Influence the Development of Chronic Diseases

Vitamin and mineral deficiency and overdose diseases are not the only health problems related to poor nutrition. Faulty diets play important roles in the development of heart disease, hypertension, diabetes, cancer, osteoporosis, dental disease, poor pregnancy outcomes, and other health problems. Poor nutrition during gestation and infancy can program lifelong increases in health problems later in life.

9. Adequacy, Variety, and Balance Are Key to Healthy Diets

Healthy diets contain many different foods that together provide calories and nutrients in amounts that promote health. Variety is a cornerstone of an adequate and balanced diet because no one food (except breast milk for young infants) provides all the nutrients we need. Most foods don't even come close to doing that.

Healthy diets are built around foods, not supplements, because there are many healthful substances in basic foods that are not available in supplements. If there is a choice between foods and supplements, you should choose foods first.

10. There Are No "Good" or "Bad" Foods

Unless you're talking about spoiled milk or poisonous mushrooms, there are no "good" or "bad" foods. People think of broccoli and whole-grain bread as good foods. You would die, however, if that's all you ate. Candy and desserts are usually labeled "bad," but limited amounts of these foods can be part of an adequate and balanced diet. Proper diets are made up of the collection of foods we eat over the course of a day or several days. It's the sum of the contributions made by individual foods that produces a diet that is either healthful or not.

Building a Healthy Diet

Take a moment to relax, close your eyes for a second, and take a deep breath. Now, give your full attention to these foods:

- A plump, golden peach. It's so ripe that juices spurt from it and drip down your chin when you take a bite.
- A Thanksgiving turkey that's still in the oven roasting, and the wonderful smell fills the whole kitchen.
- A steaming loaf of golden-brown homemade bread that has just been set out to cool.
- A perfectly ripe, just-picked tomato that melts in your mouth.

If your mouth is watering and you are ready to go out and buy some ripe peaches, you have found the balance between good taste and good for you.

Eating a healthy diet has to mean eating food you enjoy. If it doesn't, or if it's too much of a struggle, a diet won't last. Healthy diets are those people can live with and enjoy for a lifetime. The trick to starting one that will last is planning and choosing foods you like that are nutritious.

To help consumers decide what constitutes a healthy diet, the Departments of Health and Human Services and of Agriculture have developed and periodically update *Dietary Guidelines for Americans* (health.gov/dietaryguidelines). The *2005 Dietary Guidelines for Americans* provide the rationale for a healthy diet and urge Americans to:

- Eat a variety of nutrient-dense foods, including vegetables, fruits, whole-grain products, and low-fat and fat-free milk products.
- Balance caloric intake with expenditure.
- Choose foods and beverages low in saturated and trans fats, cholesterol, salt, and added sugars.

- Choose foods with monounsaturated and polyunsaturated fats and lean meats.
- Engage in regular physical activity (for about sixty minutes on most days of the week).
- Choose fiber-rich foods.
- Drink alcoholic beverages in moderation, if at all.

Chapter 11 offers you a way to translate recommendations for healthy eating into action. Recipes provided were developed by the author to deliver good taste and key nutrients needed by women before, during, and after pregnancy. Recipes for both vegetarians and meat eaters are included, and they come with an analysis of caloric and nutrient content.

MyPyramid Food Guide

How do you select the combination of foods that add up to a healthy diet? Follow the lead of the "MyPyramid" Food Guide (Figure 2.1).

The U.S. Department of Agriculture (USDA) released this version of the food selection guide in 2005. This planning tool recommends specific amounts of food from each food group based on a person's caloric need (see Table 2.8).

TABLE 2.8   MYPYRAMID DAILY FOOD INTAKE AND PHYSICAL ACTIVITY RECOMMENDATIONS AT VARIOUS LEVELS OF CALORIE NEED PER DAY

	1,800	2,000	2,200	2,400
Grains, ounces*	6	6	7	8
Vegetables, cups**	2½	2½	3	3
Fruits, cups	1½	2	2	2
Milk, cups	3	3	3	3
Meat and beans, ounces	5	5½	6	6½
Oils, teaspoons	5	5½	6	7
Other, calories	195	250	290	360

Physical Activity: At least 30 minutes of moderate intensity exercise daily

* Make half of this amount whole-grain products.

** Include dark green and other colorful vegetables.

FIGURE 2.1 MYPYRAMID FOOD GUIDE

continued

FIGURE 2.1 MYPYRAMID FOOD GUIDE, *continued*

GRAINS Make half your grains whole	VEGETABLES Vary your veggies	FRUITS Focus on fruits	MILK Get your calcium-rich foods	MEAT & BEANS Go lean with protein
Eat at least 3 oz. of whole-grain cereals, breads, crackers, rice, or pasta every day 1 oz. is about 1 slice of bread, about 1 cup of breakfast cereal, or ½ cup of cooked rice, cereal, or pasta	Eat more dark-green veggies like broccoli, spinach, and other dark leafy greens Eat more orange vegetables like carrots and sweetpotatoes Eat more dry beans and peas like pinto beans, kidney beans, and lentils	Eat a variety of fruit Choose fresh, frozen, canned, or dried fruit Go easy on fruit juices	Go low-fat or fat-free when you choose milk, yogurt, and other milk products If you don't or can't consume milk, choose lactose-free products or other calcium sources such as fortified foods and beverages	Choose low-fat or lean meats and poultry Bake it, broil it, or grill it Vary your protein routine – choose more fish, beans, peas, nuts, and seeds

For a 2,000-calorie diet, you need the amounts below from each food group. To find the amounts that are right for you, go to MyPyramid.gov.

| Eat 6 oz. every day | Eat 2½ cups every day | Eat 2 cups every day | Get 3 cups every day;
for kids aged 2 to 8, it's 2 | Eat 5½ oz. every day |

Find your balance between food and physical activity

- Be sure to stay within your daily calorie needs.
- Be physically active for at least 30 minutes most days of the week.
- About 60 minutes a day of physical activity may be needed to prevent weight gain.
- For sustaining weight loss, at least 60 to 90 minutes a day of physical activity may be required.
- Children and teenagers should be physically active for 60 minutes every day, or most days.

Know the limits on fats, sugars, and salt (sodium)

- Make most of your fat sources from fish, nuts, and vegetable oils.
- Limit solid fats like butter, stick margarine, shortening, and lard, as well as foods that contain these.
- Check the Nutrition Facts label to keep saturated fats, *trans* fats, and sodium low.
- Choose food and beverages low in added sugars. Added sugars contribute calories with few, if any, nutrients.

MyPyramid.gov
STEPS TO A HEALTHIER YOU

U.S. Department of Agriculture
Center for Nutrition Policy and Promotion
April 2005
CNPP-15

USDA is an equal opportunity provider and employer.

Source: U.S. Dept. of Agriculture and Health and Human Services

Whole-grain products, low-fat dairy products, lean meats, and a variety of colorful vegetables and fruits should be included in food choices. Table 2.9 lists these foods and others included in the groups. However, MyPyramid does not provide specific recommendations for pregnant or breast-feeding women or for vegetarians.

Diets that are based on the food groups usually have room for a serving or two a day of foods you eat mostly for fun. Because of their higher caloric needs, very physically active people and preg-

TABLE 2.9   BASIC FOOD CHOICES BY FOOD GROUP

Grains

bagels	crackers	pasta	rolls
biscuits	granola	polenta	tortillas
bread (any type)	grits	pretzels	waffles
bulgur	hot cereals	popcorn	wild rice
cold cereals	muffins	rice	
corn bread	pancakes	rice cakes	

Vegetables

asparagus	cauliflower	leeks	spinach
bean sprouts	coleslaw	lettuce (any type)	squash
beets	collard greens	lima beans	sweet potatoes
black-eyed peas	corn	mushrooms	tomatoes
broccoli	cucumber	okra	tomato juice
brussels sprouts	eggplant	onions	turnip greens
cabbage	green beans	peppers (any type)	vegetable juice
carrot juice	green peas	potatoes	watercress
carrots	kale	rutabagas	

Fruits

apple juice	cantaloupe	honeydew melon	pineapple
apples	cherries	kiwi	pineapple juice
applesauce	cranberry juice	mangoes	plums
apricots	fruit cocktail	oranges	raspberries
avocados	grapefruit	papaya	strawberries
bananas	grapefruit juice	peaches	watermelon
blueberries	grapes	pears	

Meat/Animal Products

beef (lean)	egg substitute	lobster	turkey
chicken	fish (any type)	pork	veal
crab	ham	scallops	
eggs	lamb	shrimp	

continued

TABLE 2.9   BASIC FOOD CHOICES BY FOOD GROUP, *continued*

Beans/Plant Products

dried beans	nuts	soy	tofu
hummus	peanut butter	split peas	
lentils	seeds	tempeh	

Milk

cheese (any type)	frozen yogurt	milk	yogurt
cottage cheese	ice milk	soy milk	

Other: Fats, Oils, Sweets, and Alcohol

beer	cheese	liquor	sour cream
butter	chocolate	margarine	wine
cake	cream	oil	
candy	cream cheese	salad dressing	

nant and breast-feeding women may need the calories provided by snacks and desserts.

This version of the basic food guide emphasizes physical activity. The intent is to help stem the tide of overweight and obesity in the United States. MyPyramid recommends that normal-weight individuals engage in moderate exercise for at least thirty minutes most days of the week. People who are overweight or trying to maintain a weight loss are urged to exercise for ninety minutes each day.

If you're Internet savvy, you will probably love this site. From the homepage mypyramid.gov, click on "MyPyramid Plan" and enter your age, sex, and physical activity level. (The purpose of gathering this information is to estimate your calorie requirement.) From there, a report will be generated that indicates the amount of food you should ingest from each group to consume an appropriate number of calories and an adequate diet. On this and other pages, you'll see a "MyPyramid Tracker" button. Click on it to begin an assessment of your dietary intake and physical activity level. The program will ask you to enter types and amounts of the foods and beverages you consumed in a day. The program will give you reports that specify the nutrient and food group composition of that day's diet. The physical activity assessment evaluates your physical activity status and provides related energy expenditure information and educational messages. You'll get a better indication of your dietary quality and the status of your physical activity level if you enter several days' worth of information rather than just one.

Vegetarian Diets and Precautions

"If vegetarians eat vegetables, what do humanitarians eat?" There are many variations of vegetarian diets. Some people who don't eat red meat or who eat only fish and plant foods consider themselves to be vegetarians. In its truest sense, however, a vegetarian, or vegan, diet includes only plant foods.

There are a number of benefits to eating low on the food chain. Vegetarians tend to have a lower risk of heart disease, cancer, obesity, and type 2 diabetes than meat eaters. The fact that many vegetarians do not smoke or drink alcohol excessively as well as engage in regular physical activity likely contributes to their maintenance of good health.

Vegetarian diets generally contain less protein than the average American diet, but nonetheless an adequate amount. Foods included in vegetarian diets tend to be nutrient dense, providing good amounts of fiber, vitamins, minerals, unsaturated fats, and yummy phytochemicals such as lycopene and flavanols.

There are such things as unhealthful vegetarian diets, just as is the case for omnivore diets. Vegetarian diets can contain too many high-calorie foods, like French fries, candy, desserts, pastries, and cheese. If limited in variety, vegetarian diets can lead to deficient intakes of vitamins D and B_{12}, zinc, calcium, iron, and the omega-3 fatty acids EPA and DHA. Vegetarians who do not consume products fortified with vitamin D and B_{12}, eat foods rich in EPA and DHA, or get enough sun exposure should identify sources of these nutrients in foods or supplements.

Vitamin B_{12} is only found in animal products, microorganisms, and fortified foods. Fermented foods, such as spirulina, seaweeds, and tempeh, were once thought to provide B_{12}, but they contain an inactive form of the vitamin. Vitamin D is found only in a few foods and comes to us from the sun. Ultraviolet rays from the sun convert cholesterol located in the skin to vitamin D. You can get enough vitamin D from the sun by exposing your face, arms, and legs to direct sun light for fifteen minutes twice a week. Vitamin D overdose does not occur when the source of the vitamin D is the sun. Glass and sunscreen block the sun's ultraviolet rays and the skin's manufacture of vitamin D. One other note: the intensity of the sun's rays in northern climates in the winter is insufficient for production of vitamin D. Northerners have to take a tropical vacation each winter to get their vitamin D.

Well-planned vegetarian diets are adequate for pregnant and breast-feeding women and for infants after the age of four to six months. Before that time, infants should be exclusively breast-fed or given iron-fortified infant formula.

Diagnosing the Truthfulness of Nutrition Information

Deciding whether something you read or hear about nutrition, dietary supplements, and nutritional remedies is true can be difficult. The marketplace is replete with products that promise to raise children's IQ, build muscle, melt fat, cure infection, and restore lost energy. Unlike drugs, products sold as foods or dietary supplements do not have to be tested for safety or effectiveness before they are offered to the public. Some products, such as certain herbs and high doses of vitamins and minerals, may not be safe. Although promoters of nutritional products are not supposed to make untrue claims, it happens all the time. Untested promises for dietary supplements, weight-loss aids, and herbal remedies are commonly made by salespeople. Purported benefits of nutritional products are touted on the Internet; in pamphlets, advertisements, infomercials; and on television and radio talk shows. There is little enforcement of existing regulations that prohibit bogus claims, and the mild penalties applied for wrongdoing make the risk of false statements largely worth it. Due to the lack of enforcement of protective regulations, consumers are truly on their own to decide whether what they hear or read about nutritional remedies or other products is true.

How, then, do you decide if something you read or hear about nutrition is true or, at a minimum, safe to try? Here are some suggestions for sorting out nutrition facts from fiction.

• **Be suspicious of the money motive.** Products heavily advertised in Sunday newspaper supplements, tabloids, and in-flight magazines or on radio or television that offer "new," "revolutionary," or "breakthrough" nutritional products are highly suspect. Such heavy investments in advertising spell *profit motive*. If the product worked, it wouldn't have to be oversold in such detail in advertisements. Products that offer a money-back guarantee are also suspect. Only the rare consumer returns a product even if it doesn't really work for anyone. There is no need to offer your money back if a product does what it claims to do.

• **Testimonials are a strong clue that a nutritional product is bogus.** Testimonials are worthless, regardless of what degrees or how many movies the speaker has to his or her credit. Nutritional products are a business, and people get paid to help promote them. The commonly used before-and-after photographs of people using particular weight-loss products have employed different subjects in the before and the after photographs. Well-respected scientists in areas other than nutrition have been given sizable research grants as payment for support of specific, unproven nutritional products.

• **Only objective research can determine whether a product does what is claimed.** Because many consumers are aware of this, advertisements will often announce that the product has been extensively tested and has been shown by research to work. If that is the case, write or e-mail the manufacturer and ask for a copy of the published studies. If the appropriate studies have been done, the information could be sent. Chances are excellent, however, that you will not hear back from the manufacturers who touted the scientific studies.

There are several reasons why so many untested nutritional products are available. Studies needed to test the effectiveness and safety of products are expensive. Even if they are undertaken and a product is found to be beneficial, most of the ingredients of nutritional products could not be patented. Ingredients such as vitamins, minerals, herbs, enzymes, amino acids, and algae are not unique discoveries and can be used in products by any manufacturer. Formulations of nutritional ingredients can be patented, however.

Overall, the current situation provides little incentive for manufacturers of nutritional products to invest in research. The lack of effectiveness of most of the products offered to the public ensures that there will be a continuing market for new, revolutionary formulas in the future. After all, if these remedies worked, there would be no need for additional products.

Sometimes people who represent nutritional remedies are sincere and convinced of the benefits of the products they sell despite the lack of objective proof. The problem here is that you cannot know whether the product is a bad or a good investment. You have to treat all such claims as suspect until you are shown that they are not. The standard of proof has to be the results of scientific studies. Insisting on proof that a nutritional product is safe and actually does what it is claimed to do is really not asking that much.

Reliable Sources of Nutrition Information

Not all of the nutrition information you read in newspapers, books, and magazines, find on websites, or hear on radio or television is nonsense. Many periodicals and broadcasting companies are cautious about the accuracy of information presented. This caution is exercised by investigating the reliability of the sources of nutrition information, by covering more than one side of controversial topics, and by confirming conclusions with nutrition experts before the information is presented. Some print and broadcasting companies have policies that reject advertisements that make false or deceptive nutrition claims.

Reliable nutrition information can be found in:

- Government health publications
- Information produced by scientifically recognized professional organizations, such as the American Dietetic Association, the American Institute of Nutrition, and the American Medical Association; professional and voluntary associations, such as the American Heart Association or the March of Dimes, also provide reliable nutrition information
- Articles in scientific journals that primarily publish research studies
- The Internet sites WebMD.com, Medscape.com, Mayoclinic.org, and Medlineplus.gov.
- College nutrition textbooks
- Books written by scientifically credible experts in nutrition

Other reliable sources of nutrition information exist, but it is impossible to give them blanket approval because the credibility of the data presented varies too much. For example, popular nutrition books written by people with impressive backgrounds in another field may contain hogwash, or they may be accurate. You can't tell by the credentials of the author alone. Nor can you always trust information relayed in "educational" publications produced by the food and dietary supplement industries. Infant formula companies; organizations representing the meat, wheat, potato, and dairy industries; manufacturers of vitamins and mineral supplements; and a host of other organizations publish nutrition information to promote their products. Some of these publications can be found in the waiting rooms of health-care providers. Sometimes the nutrition information conveyed is accurate, but often it is slanted in favor of the company's products. Advertisements may be included along with the articles on nutrition, and the topics selected for coverage commonly relate only to the type of food, vitamins, or other products sold by the sponsoring company.

Much of the information in this section relates to claims about nutrition and health that lie outside of what is known to be true. The truth, however, has a lot going for it—it's what you can count on.

This is the end of your "crash course" on nutrition and background information for the upcoming recommendations. If you would like to learn more about nutrition, enroll in a class at a nearby college, check out a nutrition textbook from the library, or take a self-study course. The subject is more complex than one might think, and we are learning more about it every day. Take advantage of that knowledge.

⌒ 3 ⌒

Becoming Nutritionally Prepared for the First Two Months of Pregnancy

"Everyone is kneaded out of the same dough, but not baked in the same oven."

—Yiddish proverb

U ntil recently, it was widely believed that the most important time for paying attention to nutrition was in the last half of pregnancy, when the fetus was gaining most of its birth weight. It was assumed that the importance of nutrition in pregnancy grew along with the fetus. This emphasis on nutrition later in pregnancy made sense because that is what had been studied, and its importance was clear. It was also practical, because most women did not receive prenatal care until well into pregnancy. This situation is changing as results of new studies become available and as interest in preconception and early pregnancy care grows among obstetric providers and women. New information is demonstrating that nutrition before and during the first few months of pregnancy is of more importance than had been previously imagined. The information represents an exciting advance because, if women know about it, they can apply much of this new information before they begin prenatal care.

Preconception and early pregnancy nutrition are attracting a high level of attention because of research results showing the effects of nutrition on fetal tissue and organ formation and on health long after delivery. Weight loss by the mother in the first trimester of pregnancy, for instance, may program fetal genes to conserve energy and survive on fewer calories than optimum. Later in life, the child or adult may continue to conserve calories and gain excess weight when faced with an environment that offers plenty of delicious foods. Low calcium intakes during pregnancy may increase the risk that adults will develop hypertension. Many more examples of the effects of early pregnancy nutrition and fetal programming could be mentioned.

Because most fetal tissues and organs develop within the first two months of pregnancy, waiting until pregnancy is confirmed to make changes in nutritional practices may mean opportunities are missed. To take full advantage of the benefits of good nutrition, it is best to practice optimal nutrition before conception. That way, when conception occurs, you will be nutritionally set for the critically important first months of pregnancy.

This chapter takes you on a brief tour of early fetal development and growth and describes how a woman's body changes to accommodate pregnancy. Preconception and early pregnancy nutritional practices that support optimal fetal development and growth are described, and specific recommendations given.

Anticipating Changes During the First Two Months of Pregnancy

Each of us began life as a single cell. However, that phase of life lasted a very short time. Shortly after conception, the single fertilized cell burst into action by dividing and creating new cells. By the time of birth, that single cell had multiplied into trillions of cells. Each cell did not become an exact replica of the other. Although each cell contains the same genetic material, groups of cells developed specialized functions along the way. This specialization allowed cells to form specific tissues and organs that would perform particular functions. Our brains are able to remember and to reason, and our bodies can digest food, eliminate waste, combat infection, renew bone, and perform thousands of other functions because groups of cells develop differently from other groups.

Not all tissues and organs were formed by groups of specialized cells at the same time. There was a preprogrammed time for development for every tissue and organ in our bodies. Our spinal cords, which developed into our brains, were formed within twenty-three days after conception. By thirty days after conception, in each of us a cluster of cells had formed a heart that beat weakly. Arms, legs, fingers, and toes had also taken shape by then. Within two more weeks, groups of cells had formed basic components of the liver, pancreas, stomach, ears, eyes, and lungs. All these miraculous accomplishments occurred before the cluster of cells, referred to as the *embryo*, weighed five grams, or the weight of a nickel! Each tissue and organ had to develop on schedule because there was no second chance. Development is on a very strict timetable.

For tissues and organs to form and function normally, all building materials must be present at the time tissues and organs are programmed to develop. If sufficient oxygen, water, glucose, vitamins, or minerals are not available at those times, development falters. Ill-timed exposures to medications (some anticonvulsants, antibiotics, and chemotherapeutic agents, for example), toxic agents in the environment (for instance, DDT, PCBs, mercury, lead), radiation, infectious agents, alcohol, and high levels of certain nutrients may also interrupt normal fetal development. Exposure to these insults during tissue and organ formation can result in miscarriage, malformations, or impaired physical and mental development of the fetus. The period of time during pregnancy when these exposures are most hazardous to the fetus is between implantation (approximately five days after conception) and the eight weeks following implantation.

Tissues and organs grow in size and weight after they have formed. This pattern of growth means that the major gains in fetal weight occur later in pregnancy. Once tissues and organs are formed, they are no longer vulnerable to insults that cause malformations. Insults occurring later in pregnancy, however, such as exposure to toxic substances and poor diets, may result in normally formed but undersized organs that do not function optimally.

Because there are so many factors that may affect tissue and organ development, it is almost always difficult to decide whether a specific condition was responsible for a problem occurring in an individual newborn. Not every pregnancy is affected, or affected in the same ways, by exposure to harmful substances. In addition, many of the causes of abnormal fetal development are not known. Trying to isolate a single factor that may have disrupted fetal development or growth is usually an exercise in futility for any individual pregnancy.

Despite the susceptibility of the fetus during the first few months of pregnancy, most babies are born healthy and normal. Chances are excellent, however, that mothers intend to do the most and best they possibly can for their babies during pregnancy. The shared goal is an above-average baby, one that is as healthy and as well developed as possible. The outcome cannot be guaranteed, but it can be helped along by "growing the baby in the right oven."

Changes in Your Body

A woman's body goes through major changes to accommodate pregnancy. These changes occur throughout gestation and begin in earnest shortly after conception. Within the first weeks of pregnancy, hormones that support implantation of the embryo, growth of the uterus and placenta, and expansion of the mother's circulatory system are produced in abundance. This avalanche of hormones has side effects, however. It is likely responsible for the tender and fuller breasts, cramping, nausea, vomiting, and taste and smell changes experienced by many women very early in pregnancy. Around the third month, when nausea and vomiting often subside, fatigue may set in due to an expansion in blood volume. It takes from several weeks to over a month for a woman's body to get used to the higher volume of blood in the circulatory system.

During the first half of pregnancy, while the fetus is still quite small, a number of changes take place that cause the mother to store fat and nutrients. These stores are developed early so that they will be available to support major gains in fetal weight later. A direct consequence of the tendency to increase fat stores right away is that many women feel that they are becoming "fat" rather than pregnant. As pregnancy progresses, most women will stop storing fat and use up some of what they have stored. Early gains in fat around the thighs, breasts, and trunk of the body have needlessly surprised and dismayed millions of women. Be aware: Adding fat stores is a preprogrammed phenomenon of the first half of pregnancy.

Changes in Appetite

Most women find that their hunger frequency and food intake increases earlier in pregnancy than expected. We are biologically programmed to gain weight in advance of when we need it to support major gains in fetal weight. Weight gain may also be higher than expected in the early months of pregnancy because women may eat to relieve nausea and vomiting. Other times, food intake increases simply because women get really hungry often.

Weight gain early in pregnancy concerns many women. The worry that "I'm going to gain a ton if I keep eating like this" probably arises in most everyone. The concern, however, may be misplaced. Changes in hunger and food intake during pregnancy normally come in spurts and plateaus. You may go through memorable periods of hunger and food intake one week and lose your high level of interest in eating the next. Expect that your level of hunger and food intake will vary somewhat during pregnancy, as will your rate of weight gain.

Most of the information presented about the normal course of hunger and food intake applies to pregnancies that are not complicated by restrictive eating practices, eating disorders, or exaggerated fears about weight gain. It is hard to find a woman who isn't concerned about gaining too much weight in pregnancy. However, a reasonable weight gain, which for most women should be somewhere between twenty-five and thirty-five pounds, is of critical importance to fetal development and growth. Much more is presented on the topic of weight gain and pregnancy in Chapter 6.

Changes in Taste and Smell

Ask a previously pregnant women to recall which foods tasted really good or which odors made them feel queasy when they were pregnant and you're likely to get quite a conversation going. Approximately two out of three women notice changes in the way some foods taste and smell even before they are sure they are pregnant. These changes are so distinct that they can provide a strong clue that conception has occurred. Changes in the way certain foods taste and smell are considered normal in pregnancy and are predictive of a lower-than-average risk of miscarriage.

The types of foods that tend to taste worse in pregnancy vary, but many women develop a distaste for coffee, diet sodas, and alcohol-containing beverages. Sweet and salty foods are often reported to taste better, while the smell of foods frying makes some women queasy. Avoid foods that are offensive, and, if possible, get someone else to cook if kitchen smells upset your stomach.

Specific food cravings are also known to occur in pregnancy. Some of these may be helpful, such as a craving for milk or fruit. Others, which lead to consumption of dirt, clay, or laundry starch, may be harmful.

Extreme changes in food preferences during pregnancy also occur but aren't considered normal. For example, if you make your husband or partner drive thirty miles in the middle of the night to get you watermelon, that's not a normal craving. A craving for lots of water and a desire for orange juice, soft drinks, or other sugar-rich beverages after waking up may signal a problem with glucose levels. These changes should be checked out by your health-care provider.

No inner voices direct women to consume foods that provide nutrients needed during pregnancy. Women have to make decisions about what to eat and what to avoid on their own.

Dealing with Nausea and Vomiting During Early Pregnancy

Some 70 percent of women experience nausea within the first two months of pregnancy and about half experience vomiting. These symptoms generally begin within four weeks after conception and subside by nine or ten weeks. Nausea and vomiting last throughout pregnancy in 10 to 15 percent of women. Severe or prolonged nausea and vomiting are not considered normal and should be checked out by your health-care provider.

Women who experience nausea or nausea and vomiting early in pregnancy are more than 60 percent less likely to miscarry than women who do not experience either nausea or vomiting. Increasing hormone levels that are thought to prompt nausea and vomiting may be responsible for the reduced risk of miscarriage.

It is preferable to "eat through" your nausea and vomiting rather than to lose weight. Additional information about nausea and vomiting in pregnancy and management advice are presented in Chapter 8.

Preconception and Early Pregnancy Diet

A healthy diet to bring into pregnancy is characterized by the following:

- Food intake that corresponds to the MyPyramid Food Guide eating plan
- Regular meals (no fasting or meal skipping)
- An intake of at least 400 mcg (0.4 mg) folic acid per day
- No alcohol intake
- No overuse of dietary supplements
- Enjoyment of food and mealtimes

These dietary basics apply to the first two months of pregnancy, too, but with one special consideration attached. Women should consume enough food to gain around two to four pounds during the first two months of pregnancy.

Following the MyPyramid Food Guide

The cornerstone of a healthy diet is the selection of a variety of foods that together provide the level of energy and nutrients needed for maternal health and fetal development and growth. Because many components of food that promote health are not contained in supplements, healthy diets are based around food.

The best available guide for selecting a diet that promotes preconception and early pregnancy health is the MyPyramid Guide released in 2005 (see Figure 2.1 in Chapter 2). This guide is not the same as food guides you probably learned about in school. This revision of the basic food group guide is different because it emphasizes healthy food choices at particular caloric intake levels and does not include serving sizes. People requiring 2,000 calories a day, for example, are urged to consume six ounces of grain products, two and a half cups of vegetables, one and a half cups of fruits, three cups of milk (or an equivalent amount of dairy products), and five ounces of meats or meat alternates daily. Caloric requirements of women during pregnancy vary too much to set one standard level of intake for all. The right level of calories is one that leads to an adequate rate of weight gain.

Certain types of food in the MyPyramid groups are favored over others. To emphasize their importance, the MyPyramid Guide recommends that three cups of dark green and two cups of orange vegetables be consumed weekly. Whole-grain products should make up about half of the recommended daily amount of grain products, and lean meats and low-fat dairy products are recommended choices. The MyPyramid Guide allocates 10 to 15 percent of caloric need to desserts, sweets, butter, oils, and high-fat and sugary foods.

Recommendations for physical activity are an integral part of this new guide. Along with good diets, healthy people (and pregnant women) are encouraged to engage in moderate intensity exercise (such as jogging, swimming, aerobic exercise) for at least thirty minutes daily.

Evaluating Your Diet

Some women reading this information will already be consuming the recommended diet but may not know it. Others may be concerned about what they eat and want to identify specific changes they should make. The following exercise provides assurance that a healthy diet is being consumed or will pinpoint modifications needed.

There are two ways to perform your dietary intake analysis. One can be done with paper and pencil, and the other with the mypyramid.gov website. To perform either of these evaluations, first think about your usual diet—what you customarily eat and drink. If your diet varies a good deal from day to day, pick several representative days for this exercise. Using the form provided in Figure 3.1, write down everything you eat and drink, starting with what you consumed after you awoke and continuing throughout the day until

FIGURE 3.1   USUAL DIET RECORDING FORM FOR ONE OR TWO DAYS OF FOOD INTAKE

	DAY 1		DAY 2	
Time of Day	**What I Ate and Drank**	**Amount**	**What I Ate and Drank**	**Amount**
Example:				
Noon	Chef's salad:		Vegetarian lasagna:	
	romaine	2 cups	pasta	1 cup
	turkey	1 ounce	tomato sauce	½ cup
	ham	1 ounce	zucchini	¼ cup
	cheese	1 ounce	cheese	1 ounce
	iced tea	1½ cups	milk	1 cup
Morning				
Midmorning				
Noon				
Afternoon				
Evening				
Late evening				

bedtime. Carefully measure or estimate, and record the amount of each food and beverage consumed.

To analyze your diet using the paper and pencil method, use Figure 3.2 to compare your usual intake with that recommended by the MyPyramid Food Guide. The food intake recommendations listed in Figure 3.2 are based on 2,400 calories per day. Recommendations for amounts of food in each group will be somewhat lower or higher depending on your caloric need.

First, go through the list of foods and beverages you consumed, and place each item in the appropriate food group. Foods such as gravy, mayonnaise, margarine, chips, bacon, and rich desserts and candy go into the "other" group. Foods like pretzels and popcorn, however, should go into the grain group. If you consume mixed dishes, such as pizza, stew, or burritos, break the dish into its major ingredients and sort the ingredients by group. Using Table 3.1, convert the amount of foods and beverages you consumed in each group to ounce or cup equivalents. Add up the ounces or cups of food in each food group and compare the results with the recommended amount for each group. Voilà! You have evaluated your diet.

Follow these steps to analyze your diet over the Internet.

1. Go to mypyramid.gov.
2. From the upper left-hand corner of the screen, select "MyPyramid Tracker."
3. Access the dietary analysis system by clicking on the "Check It Out" option at the bottom of the page, if you plan to use the system often, register as a New User. The U.S. Department of Agriculture (USDA) does not share records of who logs into the system.
4. Fill in requested information about age, gender, and so on. Then click on "Proceed to Food Intake."
5. Using information from your dietary intake recording sheet, enter each food item and amount and the number of times per day you consumed that amount.
6. After entering the last food item, hit the "Save and Analyze" button on the bottom of the screen.
7. From the "Analyze Your Food Intake" screen, select "Nutrient Intake." Print out this report and use it to compare your results to the recommended levels of nutrient intake given in Table 3.2.

FIGURE 3.2 EVALUATING YOUR PRECONCEPTION AND EARLY PREGNANCY DIET*

MyPyramid Guide Group	Foods and Beverages Consumed	Amount in Ounces or Cups**	MyPyramid Recommendations	Difference from Recommended Amount
1. Grains			8 ounces	
2. Vegetables			3 cups	
3. Fruits			2 cups	
4. Milk, yogurt, and cheese			3 cups	
5. Meat, poultry, fish, dry beans, eggs, and nuts			6½ ounces	
6. Fats, oils, and sweets			Fats and oils, 7 teaspoons Sweets, 1 standard serving	

* MyPyramid food group amounts are based on a 2,400-calorie food intake pattern.

** See Table 3.1 to convert other measurements into ounce and cup equivalents.

TABLE 3.1 MYPYRAMID FOOD MEASURE EQUIVALENTS

Food	Equivalents
Grains	
Bagel	1 minibagel = 1 ounce
	1 large bagel = 4 ounces
Biscuit	1 2″ diameter = 1 ounce
	1 3″ diameter = 2 ounces
Bread	1 slice = 1 ounce
Cooked cereal	½ cup = 1 ounce
Crackers	5 whole wheat = 1 ounce
	7 square/round = 1 ounce
English muffin	½ muffin = 1 ounce
Muffin	1 2½″ diameter = 1 ounce
	1 3½″ diameter = 3 ounces
Pancake	1 4½″ diameter = 1 ounce
	2 3″ diameter = 1 ounce
Popcorn	3 cups = 1 ounce
Breakfast cereal	1 cup flakes = 1 ounce
	1¼ cups puffed = 1 ounce
Rice	½ cup = 1 ounce
Pasta	½ cup = 1 ounce
Tortilla	1 6″ diameter = 1 ounce
	1 12″ diameter = 4 ounces
Vegetables	
Carrots	2 medium = 1 cup
	12 baby = 1 cup
Celery	1 large stalk = 1 cup
Corn-on-the-cob	1 6″ long = ½ cup
	1 9″ long = 1 cup
Green/red peppers	1 large = 1 cup
Potatoes	1 medium (3″ diameter) = 1 cup
Raw, leafy	2 cups = 1 cup
Tomato	1 large = 1 cup
Milk and Milk Products	
Milk	1 cup = 1 cup
Yogurt	1 cup = 1 cup
Cheese	1½ ounces hard = 1 cup
	⅓ cup shredded = 1 cup
	2 ounces processed = 1 cup
Ricotta cheese	½ cup = 1 cup
Cottage cheese	2 cups = 1 cup
Pudding	1 cup = 1 cup
Frozen yogurt	1 cup = 1 cup
Ice cream	1½ cups = 1 cup

TABLE 3.1   MYPYRAMID FOOD MEASURE EQUIVALENTS, *continued*

Food	Equivalents
Fruits	
Apple	1 small = 1 cup
	½ large = 1 cup
Banana	1 large = 1 cup
Canteloupe	⅛ melon = 1 cup
Grapes	32 grapes = 1 cup
Grapefruit	1 medium (4″ diameter) = 1 cup
Orange	1 large (3″ diameter) = 1 cup
Peach	1 large (2¾″ diameter) = 1 cup
Pear	1 medium (¼ pound) = 1 cup
Plums	3 medium = 1 cup
Strawberries	8 large = 1 cup
Watermelon	1″ wedge = 1 cup
Dried fruit	½ cup = 1 cup
Fruit juice	1 cup = 1 cup
Meats and Beans	
Steak	1 3½″ × 2½″ × ½″ = 3 ounces
Hamburger	1 small = 2 ounces
	1 medium = 4 ounces
	1 large = 6 ounces
Chicken	½ breast = 3 ounces
	1 thigh = 2 ounces
	1 leg = 3½ ounces
Pork chops	1 medium = 3 ounces
Fish	1 small can tuna = 3½ ounces
	1 small fish = 3 ounces
	1 salmon steak = 5 ounces
Seafood	5 large shrimp = 1 ounce
	10 medium clams = 3 ounces
	½ cup crab = 2 ounces
	½ cup lobster = 2½ ounces
Eggs	1 small = 1 ounce
	1 large = 2 ounces

8. At the bottom of the Nutrient Intake Analysis screen, click on "MyPyramid Recommendations." From there, you'll get a report that compares your intake with MyPyramid food group recommendations.

If your results show that you are eating according to the MyPyramid Food Guide, that is terrific! You are in a select group: Less than

TABLE 3.2   RECOMMENDED AND EXCESSIVE LEVELS OF NUTRIENT
INTAKE: PRECONCEPTION AND THE FIRST TWO MONTHS
OF PREGNANCY

Nutrient	Recommended Daily Intake	Maximum Safe Daily Intake
Vitamin A	770 mcg (2,564 IU)	3,000 mcg (10,000 IU)
Vitamin D	5 mcg (200 IU)	50 mcg (2,000 IU)
Vitamin E	15 mg (22 IU)	1,000 mg (1,490 IU)★
Vitamin K	90 mcg	—
Vitamin C	85 mg	2,000 mg
Thiamin	1.4 mg	—
Riboflavin	1.4 mg	—
Niacin	18 mg	35 mg★
Vitamin B$_6$	1.9 mg	100 mg
Folate	600 mcg	1,000 mcg★
Vitamin B$_{12}$	2.6 mcg	—
Calcium	1,000 mg	2,500 mg
Phosphorus	700 mg	3,500 mg
Magnesium	350 mg	350 mg★
Iron	27 mg	45 mg
Zinc	11 mg	40 mg
Iodine	220 mcg	1,100 mcg
Selenium	60 mcg	400 mcg
EPA + DHA	300 mg	—★★

★ Applies to levels of intake from supplements and fortified foods. For magnesium, applies to levels of intake from pharmacological agents.

★★ The FDA recommends that intakes of EPA + DHA in adults do not exceed 2,000 mg (2 g) daily from supplements.

Source: Data from Food and Nutrition Board, Institute of Medicine, National Academy of Sciences, 1997–2002; *Obstretical Gynecological Survey* 56:S1–S13, 2001.

10 percent of American adults are in this top-rated category. Here's hoping those of you who received a nutrient intake evaluation from mypyramid.gov ended up with a string of smiley faces.

If your diet is out of balance, identify specific foods you like within each food group that fell short. Then decide when you could eat those foods and what foods they should replace. Say, for example, you are short one cup from the milk, yogurt, and cheese group. Also assume you like frozen yogurt and skim milk and would enjoy eating them more often. You could decide to replace a snack such as cookies with a cup of frozen yogurt or to substitute a glass of skim milk for a soft drink.

If you would like to review a listing of foods within each basic food group to help get ideas for specific changes, refer to Table 2.9 in Chapter 2. The USDA has developed sample menus for a 2,000-calorie food pattern that shows a nutrient analysis of the menus (Figure 3.3). This information can be used to generate ideas for meal planning for yourself or your family. You can also find recipes for healthy eating in Chapter 11. The more specific plan you develop, and the more agreeable the plan is to you, the more likely it is that the changes in dietary intake will be made and sustained.

Drinking Diet Soda and Coffee

Soft drinks sweetened with NutraSweet or Equal (aspartame) and Splenda (sucralose) appear to pose no risk during pregnancy. However, diet sodas contribute little to a healthy diet.

You may want to limit coffee intake during pregnancy because of the association between intakes of over two cups of caffeinated coffee a day and miscarriage in some women. Neither coffee nor caffeine intake in pregnancy appears to be related to fetal malformations or developmental problems.

Getting Enough Folic Acid

In addition to eating a healthy diet, all women who may become pregnant should make sure they consume at least 400 mcg (0.4 mg) of the vitamin folate in the form of folic acid from prior to conception throughout pregnancy. Poor folate status during the first month of pregnancy causes about 70 percent of all cases of spina bifida and other forms of neural tube defects. Poor folate status from conception onward also increases the risk of preterm delivery, low birth weight, and fetal heart defects. Women who have had a baby with a neural tube defect and certain other types of malformations, previous miscarriages, or have delivered preterm or low-birth-weight babies should take a supplement that contains a higher amount of folic acid. Health care providers may prescribe up to 4 mg of folic acid for some women with such histories.

FIGURE 3.3 SAMPLE OF HEALTHY MENUS FROM THE U.S. DEPARTMENT OF AGRICULTURE

MyPyramid.gov
STEPS TO A HEALTHIER YOU

Sample Menus for a 2000 Calorie Food Pattern

Averaged over a week, this seven day menu provides all of the recommended amounts of nutrients and food from each food group.
(Italicized foods are part of the dish or food that preceeds it.)

Day 1

BREAKFAST

Breakfast burrito
  1 flour tortilla (7" diameter)
  1 scrambled egg (in 1 tsp soft margarine)
  1/3 cup black beans*
  2 tbsp salsa
1 cup orange juice
1 cup fat-free milk

LUNCH

Roast beef sandwich
  1 whole grain sandwich bun
  3 ounces lean roast beef
  2 slices tomato
  1/4 cup shredded romaine lettuce
  1/8 cup sauteed mushrooms (in 1 tsp oil)
  1 1/2 ounce part-skim mozzarella cheese
  1 tsp yellow mustard
3/4 cup baked potato wedges*
  1 tbsp ketchup
1 unsweetened beverage

DINNER

Stuffed broiled salmon
  5 ounce salmon
  1 ounce bread stuffing mix
  1 tbsp chopped onions
  1 tbsp diced celery
  2 tsp canola oil
1/2 cup saffron (white) rice
  1 ounce slivered almonds
1/2 cup steamed broccoli
  1 tsp soft margarine
1 cup fat-free milk

SNACKS

1 cup cantaloupe

Day 2

BREAKFAST

Hot cereal
  1/2 cup cooked oatmeal
  2 tbsp raisins
  1 tsp soft margarine
1/2 cup fat-free milk
1 cup orange juice

LUNCH

Taco salad
  2 ounces tortilla chips
  2 ounces ground turkey, sauteed in 2 tsp sunflower oil
  1/2 cup black beans*
  1/2 cup iceberg lettuce
  2 slices tomato
  1 ounce low-fat cheddar cheese
  2 tbsp salsa
  1/2 cup avocado
  1 tsp lime juice
1 unsweetened beverage

DINNER

Spinach lasagna
  1 cup lasagna noodles, cooked (2 oz dry)
  1/2 cup cooked spinach
  1/2 cup ricotta cheese
  1/2 cup tomato sauce tomato bits*
  1 ounce part-skim mozzarella cheese
1 ounce whole wheat dinner roll
1 cup fat-free milk

SNACKS

1/2 ounce dry-roasted almonds*
1/4 cup pineapple
2 tbsp raisins

Day 3

BREAKFAST

Cold cereal
  1 cup bran flakes
  1 cup fat-free milk
  1 small banana
1 slice whole wheat toast
  1 tsp soft margarine
1 cup prune juice

LUNCH

Tuna fish sandwich
  2 slices rye bread
  3 ounces tuna (packed in water, drained)
  2 tsp mayonnaise
  1 tbsp diced celery
  1/4 cup shredded romaine lettuce
  2 slices tomato
1 medium pear
1 cup fat-free milk

DINNER

Roasted chicken breast
  3 ounces boneless skinless chicken breast*
1 large baked sweetpotato
1/2 cup peas and onions
  1 tsp soft margarine
1 ounce whole wheat dinner roll
  1 tsp soft margarine
1 cup leafy greens salad
  3 tsp sunflower oil and vinegar dressing

SNACKS

1/4 cup dried apricots
1 cup low-fat fruited yogurt

Day 4

BREAKFAST

1 whole wheat English muffin
  2 tsp soft margarine
  1 tbsp jam or preserves
1 medium grapefruit
1 hard-cooked egg
1 unsweetened beverage

LUNCH

White bean-vegetable soup
  1 1/4 cup chunky vegetable soup
  1/2 cup white beans*
2 ounce breadstick
8 baby carrots
1 cup fat-free milk

DINNER

Rigatoni with meat sauce
  1 cup rigatoni pasta (2 ounces dry)
  1/2 cup tomato sauce tomato bits*
  2 ounces extra lean cooked ground beef (sauteed in 2 tsp vegetable oil)
  3 tbsp grated Parmesan cheese
Spinach salad
  1 cup baby spinach leaves
  1/2 cup tangerine slices
  1/2 ounce chopped walnuts
  3 tsp sunflower oil and vinegar dressing
1 cup fat-free milk

SNACKS

1 cup low-fat fruited yogurt

MyPyramid.gov
STEPS TO A HEALTHIER YOU

Sample Menus for a 2000 Calorie Food Pattern

Averaged over a week, this seven day menu provides all of the recommended amounts of nutrients and food from each food group.
(Italicized foods are part of the dish or food that preceeds it.)

Day 5	Day 6	Day 7
BREAKFAST	**BREAKFAST**	**BREAKFAST**
Cold cereal	French toast	Pancakes
1 cup puffed wheat cereal	*2 slices whole wheat French toast*	*3 buckwheat pancakes*
1 tbsp raisins	*2 tsp soft margarine*	*2 tsp soft margarine*
1 cup fat-free milk	*3 tbsp maple syrup*	*3 tbsp maple syrup*
1 small banana	1/2 medium grapefruit	1/2 cup strawberries
1 slice whole wheat toast	1 cup fat-free milk	3/4 cup honeydew melon
1 tsp soft margarine		1/2 cup fat-free milk
1 tsp jelly		
	LUNCH	**LUNCH**
LUNCH	Vegetarian chili on baked potato	Manhattan clam chowder
Smoked turkey sandwich	*1 cup kidney beans**	*3 ounces canned clams (drained)*
2 ounces whole wheat pita bread	*1/2 cup tomato sauce w/ tomato*	*3/4 cup mixed vegetables*
1/4 cup romaine lettuce	*tidbits**	*1 cup canned tomatoes**
2 slices tomato	*3 tbsp chopped onions*	10 whole wheat crackers*
3 ounces sliced smoked turkey	*1 ounce lowfat cheddar cheese*	1 medium orange
*breast**	*1 tsp vegetable oil*	1 cup fat-free milk
1 tbsp mayo-type salad dressing	*1 medium baked potato*	
1 tsp yellow mustard	1/2 cup cantaloupe	**DINNER**
1 cup apple slices	3/4 cup lemonade	Vegetable stir-fry
1 cup tomato juice*		*4 ounces tofu (firm)*
	DINNER	*1/4 cup green and red bell peppers*
DINNER	Hawaiian pizza	*1/2 cup bok choy*
Grilled top loin steak	*2 slices cheese pizza*	*2 tbsp vegetable oil*
5 ounces grilled top loin steak	*1 ounce canadian bacon*	1 cup brown rice
3/4 cup mashed potatoes	*1/4 cup pineapple*	1 cup lemon-flavored iced tea
2 tsp soft margarine	*2 tbsp mushrooms*	
1/2 cup steamed carrots	*2 tbsp chopped onions*	**SNACKS**
1 tbsp honey	Green salad	1 ounce sunflower seeds*
2 ounces whole wheat dinner roll	*1 cup leafy greens*	1 large banana
1 tsp soft margarine	*3 tsp sunflower oil and vinegar*	1 cup low-fat fruited yogurt
1 cup fat-free milk	*dressing*	
	1 cup fat-free milk	
SNACKS		
1 cup low-fat fruited yogurt	**SNACKS**	
	5 whole wheat crackers*	
	1/8 cup hummus	
	1/2 cup fruit cocktail (in water or juice)	

* Starred items are foods that are labeled as no-salt-added, low-sodium, or low-salt versions of the foods. They can also be prepared from scratch with little or no no added salt. All other foods are regular commercial products which contain variable levels of sodium. Average sodium level of the 7 day menu assumes no-salt-added in cooking or at the table

continued

FIGURE 3.3   SAMPLE OF HEALTHY MENUS FROM THE U.S. DEPARTMENT OF AGRICULTURE, *continued*

MyPyramid.gov
STEPS TO A HEALTHIER YOU

Sample Menus for a 2000 calorie food pattern

Averaged over a week, this seven day menu provides all of the recommended amounts of nutrients and food from each food group.
(Italicized foods are part of the dish or food that preceeds it, which is not italicized.)

Food Group		Daily Average Over One Week
GRAINS	Total Grains (oz eq)	6.0
	Whole Grains	3.4
	Refined Grains	2.6
VEGETABLES *	Total Veg* (cups)	2.6
FRUITS	Fruits (cups)	2.1
MILK	Milk (cups)	3.1
MEAT & BEANS	Meat/ Beans (oz eq)	5.6
OILS	Oils (tsp/grams)	7.2 tsp/32.4 g

*Vegetable subgroups	(weekly totals)
Dk-Green Veg (cups)	3.3
Orange Veg (cups)	2.3
Beans/ Peas (cups)	3.0
Starchy Veg (cups)	3.4
Other Veg (cups)	6.6

Nutrient	Daily Average Over One Week
Calories	1994
Protein, g	98
Protein, % kcal	20
Carbohydrate, g	264
Carbohydrate, % kcal	53
Total fat. g	67
Total fat. % kcal	30
Saturated fat, g	16
Saturated fat, % kcal	7.0
Monounsaturated fat. g	23
Polyunsaturated fat. g	23
Linoleic Acid, g	21
Alpha-linolenic Acid, g	1.1
Cholesterol, mg	207
Total dietary fiber, g	31
Potassium, mg	4715
Sodium, mg*	1948
Calcium, mg	1389
Magnesium, mg	432
Copper, mg	1.9
Iron, mg	21
Phosphorus, mg	1830
Zinc, mg	14
Thiamin, mg	1.9
Riboflavin, mg	2.5
Niacin Equivalents, mg	24
Vitamin B6, mg	2.9
Vitamin B12, mcg	18.4
Vitamin C, mg	190
Vitamin E, mg (AT)	18.9
Vitamin A, mcg (RAE)	1430
Dietary Folate Equivalents, mcg	558

* Starred items are foods that are labelled as no-salt-added, low-sodium, or low-salt versions of the foods They can also be prepared from scratch with little or no added salt. All other foods are regular commercial products which contain variable levels of sodium. Average sodium level of the 7 day menu assumes no-salt-added in cooking or at the table.

Source: mypyramid.gov/downloads/sample_menu.pdf, U.S. Dept. of Agriculture and Health and Human Services

Doses of folic acid of 1 mg or more require a prescription. The reason is because high doses of folic acid may cover up the signs of vitamin B_{12} deficiency. Although vitamin B_{12} deficiency in pregnant women is very rare, many experts recommend that vitamin B_{12} be taken along with high supplemental doses of folic acid.

You can get enough folic acid by consuming a 400 mcg folic acid supplement or by consuming folic acid–fortified breakfast cereals. Most cold breakfast cereals are fortified with 100 mcg of folic acid per serving, and several cereals (Total, Smart Start, Most, and Product 19, for example) contain 400 mcg of folic acid per serving. Check the nutrition information panel on the cereal package to confirm that the cereal you select is fortified. Breads, rice, crackers, pasta, grits, tortillas, and other refined grain products sold in the United States provide about 40 mcg of added folic acid per serving. Daily consumption of a fortified cereal along with the variety of foods recommended in the MyPyramid Food Guide will supply the needed amount of folate for most women. A list of food sources of folate is located in Appendix A.

Eating Regularly

If your usual eating pattern includes skipping meals or putting up with hunger until a convenient time to eat, this may be a good time to change it. Going without food for eight hours during the day may produce a less-than-optimal environment for early pregnancy. Eating three meals and, if needed, several snacks each day helps maintain an optimal glucose supply for the fetus. Glucose is the preferred source of energy for fetal development and growth. When we fast, blood levels of glucose drop somewhat and the fetus has to rely more heavily on fats as an energy source. Eating regular meals is also important later in pregnancy, when the fetus gains most of its birth weight. The fetus needs increasing amounts of glucose as it grows larger, and that shortens the amount of time it takes for blood glucose levels in the mother to decline.

Changing your eating pattern is more easily recommended than done. Some women do not feel hungry often or can't even think about eating in the morning. The key to change in these circumstances is to do what you find acceptable. That may mean carrying around snacks, such as peanut butter and crackers, fruit, or granola, and eating "by the clock." It may mean drinking milk or eating a slice of whole-grain toast in the morning rather than skipping breakfast altogether. As emphasized before, changes that are acceptable to you have the most staying power.

Refraining from Alcohol Intake

Heavy alcohol intake (about five or more drinks per day) early in pregnancy is associated with miscarriage and the birth of infants who are malformed, small, and mentally impaired. Infants so affected are said to have *fetal alcohol syndrome*, or FAS. Regular drinking of smaller amounts of alcohol (a drink or more per day) early in pregnancy may affect mental development and behavior. Excessive intake of alcohol later in pregnancy appears to impair growth and mental development but does not cause malformations. Adverse effects of an occasional drink in the second half of pregnancy appear to be rare. Because no amount of alcohol has been found to be absolutely safe during pregnancy, however, and to exclude the possibility of even small impairments to fetal development and growth, it is recommended that women do not drink alcohol if they may become pregnant or are pregnant.

Vitamin and Mineral Supplements and Other Considerations

Should you take a vitamin and mineral supplement before and early in pregnancy? A number of studies have shown a reduced risk of miscarriage and malformations in babies born to women taking a multivitamin and mineral supplement before and early in pregnancy. On the other hand, studies indicate that large amounts of vitamin A (over 10,000 IU per day for months at a time) and vitamin D (intakes of over 2,000 IU regularly) may harm the fetus. In a precautionary move in 1993, the American College of Obstetrics and Gynecology advised that vitamin A supplements not be used routinely during pregnancy and that, if used, not more than 5,000 IU per day should be taken. It should be mentioned that supplements of beta-carotene, a precursor of vitamin A, have not been found to cause malformations.

Women are cautioned not to eat liver more often than weekly during early pregnancy because of its high vitamin A content. They are also advised not to use Retin A or Accutane medications for acne and wrinkles because they are derived from vitamin A; their use early in pregnancy can cause miscarriage and malformations. It is best to stop use of these medications months in advance of conception.

Although common in clinical practice, use of a multivitamin and mineral supplement is not officially recommended for all pregnant women. Women who may become pregnant or are pregnant should not use high levels of vitamin and mineral supplements. Unless indicated due to a health problem, daily intake of vitamins and minerals should approximate recommended levels and not exceed maximum safe levels of intake established by the Institute of Medicine (see Table 3.2).

The decades-long practice of routinely giving all pregnant women 30 mg or more iron daily is changing, although slowly. Not all women enter pregnancy with low levels of stored iron and in need of supplemental iron. Simple and inexpensive tests for iron status can indicate who needs iron and who doesn't. The tests also indicate what levels of iron should be given. This approach, used in many European countries, spares women the unpleasant side effects that come when too much iron is given to individuals who don't need much. On the flip side of the coin are women who do need iron, and they should get it. Poor iron status during pregnancy increases the chances of preterm delivery, postpartum depression, and iron deficiency in infants. Iron supplements of 27 to 30 mg per day or more will likely be automatically given to women whose iron status is unknown or assumed to be poor.

Specific vitamin and mineral supplements may be given to women at risk of developing hypertension, preterm labor, and some other conditions during pregnancy. This topic, along with the subject of herbal supplements, is addressed in Chapter 5.

In addition, women who enter pregnancy with diabetes, hypertension, infectious disease, PKU (*phenylketonuria*, an inherited disorder), or who have had a previous baby with a congenital malformation or have a history of malformations in the family will most likely benefit from preconception and very early pregnancy care. Starting pregnancy in the best health possible can make a dramatic difference to maternal and fetal well-being.

⌒ 4 ⌒

The Right Diet
for Pregnancy

"I am only one,
But still I am one.
I cannot do everything,
But still I can do something;
And because I cannot do everything
I will not refuse to do the something that I can do."

—Edward Everett Hale, clergyman and writer

This book divides pregnancy into the early months (covered in Chapter 3) and the remaining months of pregnancy. This chapter addresses important aspects of nutrition during the last seven months of pregnancy, when fetal needs for energy and nutrients are primarily based on growth rather than on tissue and organ development. By the third month of pregnancy, most fetal tissues and organs have formed and are in the process of growing in size and complexity. A healthy diet is needed during these months primarily to support the growth of cells, maturation of the functional levels of organs, the development of the central nervous system, and the accumulation of fetal energy and the nutrient stores. During these seven months, fetal weight increases from about an ounce to approximately eight pounds.

Other components of good nutrition for pregnancy don't fall under the heading of "diet." The topics of weight gain, vitamin and mineral supplements, exercise, nutritional aids for common problems of pregnancy, and nutrition for twin pregnancies will be covered in subsequent chapters.

Major changes take place within a woman's body during these months of gestation. The changes are so dramatic that they would be considered highly abnormal if it were not for pregnancy. The amount of blood in your circulatory system, your heart rate, appetite, food intake, and weight all increase significantly. Thanks to your expanded blood supply, you may notice that your hands and feet swell up a bit, especially late in pregnancy. Most women find that their bladders don't hold as much as they used to. The nausea and vomiting of early pregnancy may suddenly disappear in these months. Constipation and heartburn may, however, take their place. In addition, a number of other bothersome but normal changes can occur during pregnancy. People who presume the "healthy glow" of pregnancy overlies internal nirvana obviously haven't been pregnant!

This chapter presents the dietary ingredients of healthy infant outcomes and highlights nutrients of particular importance to pregnancy. You will be asked to evaluate your diet and to improve your dietary intake if changes are needed. Sections on food safety and "fetal feeding" are included. The final portion of the chapter is devoted to answering questions pregnant women commonly ask about nutrition. If you have specific questions or concerns or want to discover some interesting facts about pregnancy, check out this section.

What Is a Healthy Diet for Pregnancy?

A woman's need for calories, protein, vitamins, minerals, and water all increase during pregnancy. With the exception of iron for many women, a careful selection of food can and should provide the additional calories and nutrients required. For healthy women, no special dietary supplements or foods are needed to insure adequate nutrition. What is needed is a diet that includes:

- Sufficient calories to gain weight at an appropriate rate
- The assortment of foods recommended in the MyPyramid Food Guide

- Adequate intake of all essential nutrients
- Sufficient fluid (eleven to twelve cups per day)
- A healthy dose of EPA and DHA (300 mg daily)
- Enough fiber (twenty-eight grams daily)
- No salt restriction
- No alcohol
- Foods that you enjoy and consume at pleasant mealtimes

No two women have exactly the same need for calories. That's because caloric need during pregnancy is based on an individual's physical activity level, current weight, muscle and fat mass, metabolic rate, and the stage of pregnancy. That makes it impossible to state with certainty a specific number of additional calories needed by individual pregnant women. The best way to judge the adequacy of caloric intake is by assessing weight gain.

When you consume more calories than you use up, you gain weight. When your caloric intake is lower than your body's need for calories, you lose it. In the best of all worlds, pregnant women would consume sufficient calories to consistently and gradually gain weight. The amount of weight gain that is right for pregnancy depends on prepregnancy weight and whether more than one baby is expected. (Specific information regarding weight gain is presented in Chapter 6.)

If you are eating a healthy diet and gaining weight at the recommended rate, you really don't need to worry about calories. If your weight fluctuates a bit from day to day, you shouldn't worry about that, either. Appetite and food intake levels during pregnancy come and go like the tide, only not as regularly. Good rates of weight gain often result when women eat when they are hungry and stop eating when they begin to feel full. Because this method doesn't work for all women, it may be necessary to monitor your weight gain to determine whether you are getting an adequate amount of calories.

Reevaluating Your Diet During Pregnancy: Are You Eating Healthy?

There are enough different aspects to a healthy diet in pregnancy to warrant a systematic evaluation rather than a brief, mental check.

A systematic evaluation will allow you to identify whether you're right on target or whether you need to make specific changes in your diet. If you read Chapter 3, you'll already be familiar with the dietary evaluation methods used in this book. Undertake this exercise even if you evaluated your diet earlier. Dietary intake tends to change as pregnancy progresses.

To perform this evaluation, follow the instructions given in Chapter 3 for recording, evaluating, and modifying (if needed) your dietary intake. Tips for improving intake of key nutrients for pregnancy are presented later in this chapter. Clean copies of forms for recording and analyzing your dietary intake are provided here (see Figures 4.1 and 4.2). Then complete a quick assessment of your intake of EPA and DHA—the important omega-3 fatty acids that aren't included in the standard assessment methods.

Getting Enough Fluids

Most women need about eleven to twelve cups of fluid daily during pregnancy. This amount of fluid is usually obtained from beverages and foods that are part of the regular diet. Women tend to consume as much fluid as they need because the body has internal mechanisms that signal "I'm thirsty" when the body is running short on water. These internal mechanisms, however, may not make individuals thirsty enough when the need for water is high. Pregnant women who are exposed to hot, humid climates may fail to consume enough fluid if they depend on the "I'm thirsty" internal signal. Getting enough fluids is also a concern for women who experience vomiting in pregnancy. In these situations, women are urged to regularly drink fluids such as water or diluted fruit juice. It will help keep your energy level up and the chances of developing dehydration down.

Consuming Enough High-Fiber Foods

Constipation is a common problem in pregnancy that can often be prevented by high-fiber diets. High-fiber foods are generally good sources of a variety of nutrients, so they are good to eat even if constipation isn't a problem.

How much fiber is enough to prevent constipation? For pregnant women, it's 28 g a day. Where do you get fiber? Table 2.3 listed

**FIGURE 4.1   USUAL DIET RECORDING FORM FOR ONE OR TWO DAYS OF
                FOOD INTAKE**

	Day 1		Day 2	
Time of Day	**What I Ate and Drank**	**Amount**	**What I Ate and Drank**	**Amount**
Example:				
Noon	Chef's salad:		Vegetarian lasagna:	
	romaine	2 cups	pasta	1 cup
	turkey	1 ounce	tomato sauce	½ cup
	ham	1 ounce	zucchini	¼ cup
	cheese	1 ounce	cheese	1 ounce
	iced tea	1½ cups	milk	1 cup
Morning				
Midmorning				
Noon				
Afternoon				
Evening				
Late evening				

FIGURE 4.2   EVALUATING YOUR PREGNANCY DIET*

MyPyramid Guide Group	Foods and Beverages Consumed	Amount in Ounces or Cups**	MyPyramid Recommendations	Difference from Recommended Amount
1. Grains			8 ounces	
2. Vegetables			3 cups	
3. Fruits			2 cups	
4. Milk			3 cups	
5. Meat and beans			6½ ounces	
6. Oils			7 teaspoons	
7. Other			1 standard serving	

* MyPyramid food group amounts are based on a 2,400-calorie food intake pattern.

** See Table 3.1 in Chapter 3 to convert other measurements into ounce and cup equivalents.

food sources of fiber. Choose the sources you like and can fit into your diet. Powdered, supplemental fiber you can buy in many pharmacies and grocery stores also works. (Fiber pills are not recommended because of their size.) If you use powdered fiber, follow the directions on the container. Individuals vary a good deal in their sensitivity to fiber. An overdose may cause diarrhea, and, if too little water is consumed, fiber can be constipating. Water allows fiber to swell and create the bulk that stimulates the movement of waste products along the intestinal tract. You know you have consumed the right amount of fiber when your stools are soft and well formed.

Restricting Alcohol but Not Salt

The American College of Obstetrics and Gynecology advises that restricting salt intake during pregnancy is not beneficial and may be harmful. Women should not restrict salt or sodium intake during pregnancy. Women who enter pregnancy with hypertension may need to watch their salt and sodium intake carefully. These women should obtain specific recommendations on salt and sodium intake from their health-care providers.

It is recommended that pregnant women refrain from drinking alcohol-containing beverages because alcohol may harm the fetus. If you would like additional information about this topic, refer to Chapter 3.

Enjoying Foods You Like

We have something to learn from Japanese dietary guidelines. The last guideline states: "Make all activities pertaining to food and eating pleasurable ones." All-too-busy Americans sometimes forget about the joy of eating good food with family and friends. Take the time to devote your attention to the foods you eat and to enjoy mealtimes. Bon appétit!

Key Nutrients for Pregnancy

It is important to consume enough of every nutrient required during pregnancy. Certain nutrients, however, deserve a spotlight because they are most likely to be present in low amounts in the diets of pregnant women.

Folic Acid

Folic acid, which I mentioned briefly in the previous chapter, is a synthetic form of the B vitamin folate that has gained prominence as a vitamin you need in ample amounts prior to and during pregnancy. Consumption of an adequate amount of folic acid helps prevent fetal growth abnormalities, preterm delivery, and low-birth-weight newborns. Folate, the naturally occuring form of the vitamin, also performs these functions but not as efficiently as does folic acid. Recommended folate intake during pregnancy is 600 mcg daily, of which 400 mcg should come from folic acid.

Folate means *foliage*. It was first discovered in spinach and is found in many vegetables, especially those that are leafy and green. Broccoli, oranges, bananas, milk, and dried beans are good sources of folate. Vegetables and fruits provide an average of 42 mcg of folate per serving. Breakfast cereals are often fortified with folic acid, and refined grain products, such as bread, grits, white rice, crackers, and pasta, are, by law, fortified with folic acid. Each serving of these grain products provides approximately 40 mcg of folic acid. The amount of folic acid added to breakfast cereals varies. Some whole-grain cereals aren't fortified, whereas other cereals contain 100 to 400 mcg per serving. Buy breakfast cereals with at least 100 mcg folic acid per serving.

If you consume five servings of fruits and vegetables daily along with a serving of fortified breakfast cereal and six servings of grain products, your total folate intake will likely be at least 600 mcg—the recommended amount.

Vitamin B$_{12}$

Vitamin B$_{12}$ and folate work together to help form fetal tissue and organs. On average, pregnant women consume twice as much vitamin B$_{12}$ as they need. (Here comes the big *but*.) BUT, women who don't eat animal products or who eat a very limited amount of them are at risk for B$_{12}$ deficiency. If that is you, read on.

Vitamin B_{12} is found only in animal products such as pork, chicken, eggs, and milk. It is added to some types of plant products, thereby giving vegans and near-vegans a variety of food choices for vitamin B_{12}. Foods that may be fortified with nonanimal sources of B_{12} include a specific type of nutritional yeast (Red Star T6635), soy and rice milks, and breakfast cereals. Check the nutrition information labels and aim for getting about 2.6 mcg of vitamin B_{12} of daily.

Vitamin D

Vitamin D supports fetal growth, the addition of calcium to bone, and tooth and enamel formation. Lack of it compromises fetal growth and bone development, and this may be happening during many pregnancies. About 42 percent of African-American and 4 percent of Caucasian women have low blood levels of vitamin D. Vegan women may also be a risk for poor vitamin D status because vitamin D is naturally present only in animal products.

An intake of 5 mcg (200 IU) vitamin D daily is officially recommended for pregnancy. Some credible experts, however, assert that more vitamin D than that is needed. It would not be surprising to see recommended intake levels of vitamin D double. However, you should not be getting more than 50 mcg (2,000 IU) of vitamin D daily from foods and supplements.

A great source of vitamin D is sunshine. Ultraviolet rays from the sun convert cholesterol in the skin to vitamin D. People with light skin wearing a bathing suit for one-half hour on a sunny, summer afternoon produce about 1,250 mcg (50,000 IU) vitamin D. Individuals with dark skin need two to five times this length of sun exposure to produce that much vitamin D. Two fifteen-minute sunbathing sessions per week provide plenty of vitamin D and a low risk of sunburn in most people. There is no evidence that vitamin D overdose occurs due to sun exposure.

Clothing, sunscreen, and windows block ultraviolet rays from reaching the skin and prevent vitamin D production. Exposing skin to the weak rays of the sun during the winter in cold climates doesn't produce much, if any, vitamin D, either. To prove the point, a professor in Boston sent several scantily clad graduate students to a rooftop to sunbathe for awhile in the middle of winter. The results: all the students got was cold. The sunlight was too weak to produce any vitamin D whatsoever in their skin.

Foods supply vitamin D, but the list of sources is short (see Appendix A). Milk in the United States is fortified with 2.5 mcg (100 IU) vitamin D per cup and is the leading dietary source. Vitamin D fortification of foods is becoming increasingly popular due to relaxed regulations governing the addition of vitamin D to foods. If you are concerned about your vitamin D status, check the nutrition information labels on food products, and determine if you're spending enough time in the sun.

Calcium

A lack of calcium in the mother's diet doesn't jeopardize fetal bone growth as does inadequate levels of vitamin D. If a woman's intake of calcium is low, calcium from the mother's bones will be used to meet fetal needs for calcium. There is evidence that low calcium intake may be involved in the development of hypertension during pregnancy.

Calcium is a key concern for women who don't consume three or more servings per day of dairy products or calcium-fortified soy or rice milk or eat plenty of vegetables sources of calcium daily. Obtaining the recommended level of calcium intake during pregnancy of 1,000 mg per day is very difficult if these foods are not consumed. Appendix A provides a list of food sources that may be helpful in identifying foods you could eat to meet your need for calcium. When you think of calcium, you should automatically think about vitamin D. You need vitamin D for calcium absorption and the incorporation of calcium into bone.

Iron

Women have a high need for iron during pregnancy because it is used to form a large quantity of hemoglobin and is required for fetal growth. That is why the recommended intake level for iron in pregnancy is a whopping 27 mg. Most women consume about half that amount, and it is common for women to conceive without sufficient stores to cover the iron cost of pregnancy. Consequently, iron supplementation during pregnancy is routine in many clinical practices.

It is possible for women to get enough iron from their diets, but it takes a careful selection of food. One of the easiest ways to obtain iron from the diet is to consume a highly fortified breakfast cereal (such as Product 19, Most, Smart Start, or Total). These cereals are fortified with 18 mg of iron per serving. Many other breakfast cereals are fortified with 4 or more mg of iron per serving. The absorption of iron from cereals can be doubled or tripled if consumed with a source of vitamin C, such as orange or grapefruit juice. Absorption of iron from plant foods, such as kale, turnip greens, collard greens, asparagus, black-eyed peas, dried beans, and spinach, is also increased substantially if foods high in vitamin C are consumed at the same meal. Appendix A lists good food sources of iron and vitamin C. Absorption of iron from meats is more complete than that from plants. On average, a three-ounce serving of red meat (about the size of a deck of cards) supplies 3 mg of iron, and a three-ounce serving of fish or poultry, 1 mg of iron. Liver is an excellent source of iron (providing 7.5 mg per three ounces), but because it contains very high amounts of vitamin A, it should be consumed no more than once a week.

Cast-iron pans are a good source of iron because some of the iron in the pan is absorbed by the food during cooking. Although it is hard to say how much iron you get from the pan, it is likely to be several milligrams or more per serving of food cooked for ten to fifteen minutes. Acidic foods, like tomatoes and applesauce, leach more iron from iron pans than do foods such as potatoes or eggs. If you're a newcomer to using a cast-iron pan, make sure you "season" it first. Chapter 11 lets you know how to do that.

Although healthy pregnant women require 27 mg iron per day, many prenatal supplements contain far more than that amount (45 to 60 mg). The use of high doses of iron, especially in women who have good iron stores, causes gas, cramps, and constipation and may decrease zinc absorption. The practice of giving high doses of iron routinely to pregnant women is considered "old school." Doses of iron over 27 mg daily should be given as indicated for iron deficiency or iron deficiency anemia, not routinely.

Zinc

Adequate zinc levels in pregnancy help women resist infectious diseases, may help prevent abnormally long labor, and support fetal growth. The recommended intake of zinc during pregnancy is 11 mg daily, and one in two women consume less than that amount. Zinc and iron are found in many of the same foods (meats, fortified breakfast cereals, and dried beans).

Iodine

Iodine is needed for normal thyroid function and plays important roles in protein tissue construction and maintenance. A lack of iodine during pregnancy can interfere with fetal development and, in extreme cases, cause mental and growth retardation and malformations in children.

About half of American pregnant women consume less than the recommended 220 mcg of iodine daily. The most reliable source of iodine is iodized salt. One teaspoon contains 400 mcg iodine. Salt with added iodine is clearly labeled as "Iodized." Fish, shellfish, seaweed, and some types of tea also provide iodine (see the last page of Appendix A for a list of food sources). Iodine also ends up in foods manufactured in plants that use iodine-containing solutions to clean equipment. Women who consume iodized salt are not likely to need supplemental iodine. Usual iodine intake should not exceed 1,100 mcg daily during pregnancy.

Antioxidants

One of the most convincing arguments for getting nutrients you need from foods rather than supplements is the fact that foods provide specific phytochemicals (plant chemicals) that benefit health and reproduction. Some phytochemicals are natural pigments, and others protect plants from insects and diseases. Many of the pigments act as antioxidants, protecting plant cells and their DNA from damage due to exposure to oxygen. A wide array of these plant pigments have the same antioxidant effects in humans. During pregnancy, these antioxidant pigments promote maternal health by reducing inflammation. They also help protect the cells of the developing fetus. Vitamins C and E found in plants also perform important antioxidant roles during pregnancy.

Foods rich in antioxidant pigments advertise that fact by their color. Look for beautiful red, orange, dark green, deep yellow, and blue-purple fruits and vegetables. They are loaded with yummy antioxidants. Many of these same foods are rich in vitamin C. For vitamin E, you'll need to switch gears and go to the section of the market where nuts, seeds, and oils are sold.

Vitamin A—Getting Enough, But Not Too Much

Vitamin A represents a classic case of how too little or too much of a good thing can be bad. It is needed during pregnancy for development of the fetal heart, central nervous system, circulatory and respiratory systems, and bones. Too little vitamin A can result in malformations, and so can too much. Almost half of American pregnant women consume less than 770 mcg (2,564 IU) daily, the recommended amount. A much smaller proportion of women consume too much of it.

Your dietary assessment results will let you know if you are getting too little vitamin A from food (less than 770 mcg daily). Consumption of over 3,000 mcg (10,000 IU) per day as preformed vitamin A is considered too much. Preformed vitamin A is found in animal products such as liver and eggs and in medications used for acne and wrinkles. Supplements, fortified foods, and medications containing retinol, retionic acid, retinyl palmitate, and retinyl acetate provide preformed vitamin A. Supplements and medications containing high doses of preformed vitamin A *should not* be used by women who are or may become pregnant. Use should stop at least three months prior to conception.

Vitamin A is also made in the body from beta-carotene, a plant pigment. High intakes of beta-carotene do not lead to the production of excess vitamin A in the body. Beta-carotene is considered the preferred form of the vitamin for use in food fortification and supplements. Beta-carotene is bright orange and is found in vegetables and fruits such as pumpkin, carrots, and sweet potatoes as well as in dark green, leafy vegetables.

Protein

Dietary protein provides the building blocks for fetal tissue and organs. Protein is a key component of enzymes, red blood cells, bones, and many other body parts. It deserves its reputation as being a very important nutrient for pregnant women. On average, however, women consume more protein than is required for pregnancy. The relatively high average intake of protein by pregnant women does not tell the whole story. One in four women consume less than the recommended seventy-one grams of protein.

Protein is found in good amounts in meats, milk, cheese, eggs, and dried beans. It is also present in modest amounts in grain products. You can use the information on the protein content of food in Table 2.4 to quickly estimate how much protein you consume daily.

Protein powders and supplements are not recommended for pregnancy because they may stunt fetal growth. High-protein (low-carbohydrate) diets aren't recommended, either. High-protein diets usually provide low amounts of folic acid, vitamin C, fiber, and other specific nutrients. Excess dietary protein disrupts protein tissue construction and interferes with normal fetal development.

EPA and DHA

EPA and DHA, two omega-3 fatty acids, are becoming the folic acid of the recent past. New research is quickly informing us of their roles in fetal and infant development and of the benefits of consuming adequate amounts of them. EPA (*eicosapentaenoic acid*) and DHA (*docosahexaenoic acid*) are long-chain, highly unsaturated fatty acids that promote maternal health and support the optimal development of vision and the central nervous system of the fetus and infant. Women who have adequate EPA and DHA intake during pregnancy and breast-feeding tend to deliver infants that develop a somewhat higher level of intelligence, better vision, and otherwise more mature central nervous system functioning than do infants born to women with low intake of EPA and DHA. Rates of preterm delivery are significantly lower among women with adequate EPA and DHA status.

It is currently recommended that women consume a total of 300 mg of EPA + DHA daily during pregnancy and breast-feeding. Most pregnant and breast-feeding women in the United States consume less than one third of this amount.

EPA and DHA are found together in fish, fish oils, and seafood (it turns out that fish really *is* brain food); DHA is available in omega-3-fortified eggs ("Omega Eggs"). EPA and DHA are also available in supplements, as both can be extracted from fish oils and DHA can be produced by microalgae.

Unfortunately, some types of fish are contaminated with mercury and other pollutants that may adversely affect fetal mental development. Consequently, eating fish during pregnancy and breastfeeding should be limited to twelve ounces or less per week. Certain types of large, predatory fish with high mercury content (swordfish, tilefish, shark, and king mackerel) *should not* be eaten at all by pregnant and breast-feeding women. In general, wild (rather than farm-raised) and canned fish have the lowest levels of mercury. Many types of small, nonpredatory fish (less than twenty inches) and shellfish, however, contain only trace amounts of mercury and a good supply of EPA and DHA. These fish and shellfish, and other sources of EPA and DHA, are listed in Table 4.1.

Food Safety During Pregnancy

Certain food-born illnesses can have devastating consequences during pregnancy due to their effects on the fetus. The two most important of these food born illnesses are *listerosis*, caused by *listeria monocytogenes*, and *toxoplasmosis*, due to an infection from *toxoplasma gondii*.

Infection with listeria bacteria during pregnancy is associated with miscarriage, stillbirth, and vision problems in children. Listeria is found in soil and feces of animals and humans who carry the bacteria. Listerosis can develop from consumption of any food that has come into contact with *listeria* bacteria. Most commonly, it is

TABLE 4.1   SAFE FOOD SOURCES OF EPA AND DHA*

Source	EPA + DHA, mg
Herring, 3½ ounces	1,000–1,800
Salmon, 3½ ounces	1,000–1,800
Anchovies, 3½ ounces	1,400
Whitefish, 3½ ounces	1,300
Halibut, 3½ ounces	400–900
Shrimp, 3½ ounces	500
Pollock, 3½ ounces	500
King crab, 3½ ounces	400
Lobster, 3½ ounces	400
Cod, 3½ ounces	300
Haddock, 3½ ounces	200
Perch, 3½ ounces	200
Clams, 3½ ounces	100
Other	
Egg yolk, 1	40
DHA-fortified egg, 1	150–300
Human milk, 3½ ounces	200
Supplements	100+

* Mercury content of a serving assessed at <0.2 ppm

Sources: Purdue University, http://fn.cfs.purdue.edu, 2004; http://vm.cfsan.fad.gov/~frf/sea-mehg.html, 2001.

spread by meat, fish, and unpasteurized milk, soft cheeses, and other dairy products. To prevent infection, women should not eat raw or undercooked meat, fish, or eggs or unpasteurized dairy products. Hands should be washed thoroughly before food handling.

Toxoplasma gondii is a protozoa found in soil and the feces of infected animals and humans. It can end up on or in foods such as eggs and meat that come into contact with animal feces at processing plants. You can become infected with toxoplasma through air when you clean a litter box containing contaminated feces. Toxoplasmosis infection during pregnancy can cause mental retardation, seizures, and death in a fetus and health disorders later in the child's life. Prevention of toxoplasmosis involves:

- Wearing gloves when you garden
- Washing your hands thoroughly before handling food

- Cleaning vegetables and fruits before you eat them
- Not eating raw or undercooked meats or eggs
- Having someone else clean the litter box if your pet is allowed outdoors

Food safety is an important issue during pregnancy. Basic rules of safe food handling and storage, however, should be followed on a day-to-day basis. You'll find solid information about food safety listed in the Additional Resources section for this chapter at the end of the book.

Nourishing Your Growing Baby

Only well-nourished women are in a position to optimally nourish a fetus. That is because when you eat, the nutrients consumed in foods do not go directly to the fetus. The body processes the nutrients by first changing them into forms the body can use. After nutrients are processed by the body and made available for use, the mother's needs for them are generally met first. For example, if a woman's iron stores are low or if too little vitamin D is available, the incoming supply of iron or vitamin D first will be used to meet the mother's needs. When the mother's need for iron or vitamin D is met, the placenta gets priority on the available nutrient supply. When the placenta has a sufficient supply of nutrients to grow and function normally, then the fetus is given access to available nutrients. The bottom line is that the fetus does not get "first dibs" on nutrients supplied by the mother's diet. The priority system of favoring the mother's nutrient supply over that of a fetus makes sense biologically. Mother Nature is favoring the health of the reproducer. For optimal fetal growth, diets during pregnancy must meet the needs of both the mother and the fetus.

Questions About Diet and Pregnancy

This section addresses many of the questions commonly asked by pregnant women. The questions are divided into five categories:

- General diet
- Foods to eat or avoid

- Appetite and food cravings
- Diet and changes in a woman's body
- Fun facts about pregnancy

Some of these were touched on in earlier chapters and some will be covered in more detail in later chapters, but here's a brief glimpse at the more common questions I've addressed over the years.

General Diet

How much should I eat during pregnancy?

Enough to gain weight at the appropriate rate. The amount of food a woman should consume during pregnancy varies by her level of physical activity and other factors. There is no one amount of weight to gain that's right for everyone. If you are concerned, the best way to judge whether you are eating enough or too much is to monitor your weight gain using the information provided in Chapter 6.

How do I know if I'm eating enough for the baby?

You can usually know by your weight gain. If your weight gain is on target, you most likely are eating enough for the baby. Sometimes women will gain a good deal of weight (two or more pounds in a week) even though they are not eating that much. The gain may be due to water retention. Women who are retaining water may have swelling, or *edema*, in their lower legs and hands. In this case, you can't count on your weight as being a good indicator of whether you are eating enough or too much. Eating basic foods to satisfy your appetite, or at least not restricting your food intake, may be your best guide in this situation.

I was heavy before pregnancy. Do I need to eat as much as other women?

You need to eat enough to maintain a gradual gain in weight. If you started pregnancy with a BMI over 30, you should gain around half a pound per week. Pregnancy is not the time to lose weight, no matter what your prepregnancy weight was.

I'm a vegan. Is there anything special I should do?

A well-planned vegan diet is a healthy one for pregnancy. It is prudent, however, to assess your intake of vitamin B_{12}, vitamin D, EPA and DHA, calcium, iron, and zinc, as well as to monitor your weight gain. Some soy and rice milks and many breakfast cereals are fortified with some of these key nutrients. You should check the nutrition information labels to be sure, however. A multivitamin and mineral supplement can be used if needed.

Won't the baby just take what it needs from me, regardless of what I eat?

The fetus does not act like a parasite. What you eat is important. The mother's diet and nutrient stores need to be adequate to meet her own needs as well as those of the growing fetus. Infants have been born with various vitamin deficiency diseases to women who show no signs of deficiency.

Won't my body tell me what foods to eat during pregnancy?

There is no inner voice that directs women to a nutritious diet during pregnancy. Women make those decisions based on years of learning experiences involving foods.

Should I watch my fat intake?

Pregnancy does not appear to be the time to go on a low-fat diet. A low-fat diet may interfere with getting enough calories and may deprive the fetus of certain types of fats that are needed for fetal development. Trans fats are best avoided because they may impair fetal development.

I'm not eating that much more than I did before pregnancy, yet I'm gaining weight. How can that happen?

That may happen, especially during the first few months of pregnancy, when women tend to tire easily. It is probably due to a decrease in physical activity. Many women reduce their levels of physical activity during pregnancy while not changing their food intake very much. Calories saved from a lower expenditure of energy on physical activity can contribute to weight gain.

Should I ask for a referral to, or make an appointment with, a dietitian/ nutritionist during pregnancy?

The answer is "yes" for women who:

- Doubt that the information or advice they have been given about nutrition is accurate
- Have been given insufficient information about a nutritional concern to be able to make the appropriate change
- Have gestational diabetes or have entered pregnancy with a disorder such as PKU, chronic renal disease, diabetes, or an eating disorder; have problems gaining weight or eating a healthy diet; or are on a restrictive diet

Perinatal dietitians/nutritionists specialize in pregnancy and are your best resource. Many managed care organizations have dietitians/nutritionists on staff, and most insurance companies will reimburse the costs for services of a bona fide dietitian/nutritionist with a doctor's referral or sometimes upon a patient's request. If there is a question about coverage, call your insurance provider. If you don't have medical insurance, call your local health department and ask to speak with a nutritionist who knows about pregnancy.

Our family has run into tough times, and we don't have enough money for food. Can we get help?

Yes. The first step is to call your local health department and ask about food and nutrition assistance programs. Many communities have food pantries, free meal programs, Second Harvest programs, and other types of assistance available. If your yearly household income is low, you may be eligible for the "WIC" program. This food and nutrition education program is specifically designed for low-income pregnant women and children at nutritional risk.

Is it okay to drink or eat during labor?

It depends on whom you ask. Some health-care providers insist that women should not eat or drink during labor, while others think it's a myth. The primary reason for not allowing fluids and food during labor is related to the possible use of general anesthesia. If general anesthesia is used for a surgical delivery, vomiting may occur and some of the contents of the stomach may be inhaled into the lungs. This can cause serious problems. On the other hand, some health-care providers allow women to drink fluids or to eat light foods during labor if the likelihood is extremely low that general anesthesia will be used. They believe that allowing fluid and food helps keep the woman hydrated and may help prevent fatigue. Going through the active part of labor on a full stomach is probably like eating a big meal right before you swim the English Channel; it is not a good idea.

Foods to Eat or Avoid

I don't like fish and don't want to eat those "doctored" eggs. Anyplace else I can get EPA and DHA?

Your choices are limited. You can take EPA and DHA in the form of a purified fish oil supplement, get DHA from a micro-algae supplement, or eat shellfish (see Table 4.1).

Can I get EPA and DHA from flaxseed or walnut oil? I know they are good sources of the omega-3 fatty acid alpha-linolenic acid.

These and other plant sources of alpha-linolenic acid are not good sources of EPA and DHA. Although some of the alpha-linolenic acid in flaxseed, walnuts, walnut oil, and dark, leafy green vegetables is converted by the body to EPA and DHA, the amount is very limited.

Which oils are considered healthful?

Oils high in monounsaturated fats (olive, canola, safflower, walnut, and flaxseed oils) and EPA and DHA,

Is a raw-food diet okay for pregnant women?

No, and here's why. Raw-food diets are usually low in calories, protein, and certain vitamins and minerals. Some of the foods included in this type of diet can be sources of food-borne illnesses.

Don't tell me chocolate is bad for you. It isn't, is it?

No, it's actually good. Dark chocolate is rich in flavanols—phytochemicals that help the body utilize glucose. As an occasional treat, go for it. Try the hot fudge sauce included in the recipes in Chapter 11.

Can I eat black licorice?

Only in very small amounts, if at all. Black licorice contains glycyrrhizin (no kidding), a substance that can prompt preterm labor when consumed in excess.

Do I have to drink milk?

No. But you do need to make sure you get enough calcium and vitamin D. Milk is a nutrient-dense food that is hard to replace in the diet. If you can drink milk, you should. Low-fat chocolate milk is an option for women who will drink it but not regular milk. Orange juice fortified with calcium and vitamin D is also a good choice.

Dairy products give me gas and cramps, so I don't eat them. What other foods can I eat to get enough calcium?

You may have lactose intolerance (like most adults worldwide). If so, you can consume low-lactose milk and probably yogurt, or you can take a lactase pill before you eat dairy products; however, lactase pills tend to be quite expensive.

Many, but not all, people with lactose intolerance can eat small amounts of dairy products with few or no side effects. You may be able to drink a cup or a half-cup of milk or eat an ounce of cheese at a meal and feel no discomfort. Many types of yogurt contain little lactose and are easily digested. No-lactose milks are widely available, and you could try appropriately fortified soy or rice milk.

Another reason some people don't tolerate dairy products well is an allergy to cow's milk protein. This condition is rare in adults, but, if it exists, substituting no-lactose milk for regular milk won't relieve the unpleasant symptoms. Supplemental calcium and vitamin D may be the best alternative if you are allergic to milk and dairy products.

Do spicy foods hurt the baby?

No. Components of spicy foods that end up in the mother's blood are not harmful to the fetus. They may give you gas, though.

Should I avoid food additives while I'm pregnant?

Food additives that weren't a problem before you conceived should not become one during pregnancy. In general, food additives are considered safe.

Is it okay to drink diet sodas if you are pregnant?

They appear to be safe.

Is it okay to drink herbal teas?

Maybe yes and maybe no. If this question is important to you, read the section on herbal remedies in Chapter 5.

I'm over halfway through my pregnancy. Will an occasional drink of wine or beer hurt the baby?

Probably not, but it is still best not to drink. It appears that a drink or two a week from midpregnancy on may not damage the fetus in an easily noticeable way. However, harmful effects cannot be ruled out. One study found that as little as one drink a day in pregnancy was related to attention deficit disorder in children at age fourteen. When a pregnant woman has a drink, so does her fetus. Alcohol is rapidly transported from the mother's blood to that of the fetus. To be on the safe side, it is better not to drink at all during pregnancy.

Will it harm my baby if I drink coffee during pregnancy?

Coffee consumption in the first two months of pregnancy is weakly related to the risk of miscarriage. However, drinking coffee after the first two months does not appear to harm the baby, and drinking several cups of coffee per day is considered safe. Coffee intake has not been associated with the development of malformations in the baby nor with health or behavioral problems later in childhood.

I don't want to become anemic, but I don't like taking my iron pills. Are there foods I can eat that will prevent anemia?

Yes, there are, and they were presented under "Iron" in this chapter. The requirement for iron increases a good deal in pregnancy, and it may be difficult to get enough iron without taking a supplement. Women who enter pregnancy with a good supply of stored iron and who consume foods high in iron and vitamin C maintain better iron levels than women who conceive with low iron stores and who take in few sources of iron and vitamin C. If iron levels become low, an iron supplement in a dose that can be easily tolerated should be used starting as early in pregnancy as possible. Low doses of iron (20 to 30 mg per day) are generally much better tolerated than are higher doses.

Are certain vegetables, like strong-tasting ones, bad for your baby?

Claims that certain vegetables, such as broccoli, brussels sprouts, cabbage, garlic, and cauliflower, make women nauseous or harm their fetuses have not been shown to be true. Eat the variety of vegetables you like. They really are good for you and the baby.

Should I cut back on salt?

Pregnant women in general should not restrict their salt intake. The practice of routinely restricting the salt intake of pregnant women hasn't completely faded away in this and other countries, although it is not a good idea. Salt restriction may actually be harmful and is associated with a poorer-quality diet, reduced weight gain, and the birth of underweight infants. There is no evidence that salt restriction helps reduce high blood pressure that develops in pregnancy. Salt restriction may actually aggravate problems with blood pressure. Although pregnant women should not eat salt to excess, it should be consumed "to taste." Many women find that their desire for salt and salty foods increases somewhat during pregnancy. That is a normal change.

Women entering pregnancy with hypertension that was partially controlled by a salt-restricted diet should maintain a diet that is slightly less restrictive of salt than the prepregnancy one. That is because pregnant women have an increased need for sodium. Women with preexisting hypertension should work closely with their health-care provider on the control of their blood pressure during and after pregnancy.

Appetite and Food Cravings

My appetite isn't that good. What can I do about it?

If you're not gaining weight and your appetite has been poor for more than a week, you may have to eat by the clock rather than by your appetite. That means eating meals at regular times and carrying around snacks. Small, frequent meals sometimes go down easier than large ones in women with poor appetites. You should contact your health-care provider if you try but can't gain weight. If the poor appetite is due to nausea or vomiting during pregnancy, go to Chapter 8 for specific advice.

The other morning at breakfast I ate six big pancakes. They tasted delicious but I'm usually stuffed after two. What's happening?

You have entered the "hunger zone." Periods of above-average hunger and food intake are characteristic of periods of growth. You shouldn't worry too much about it. Hunger periods come and go.

Ever since I became pregnant, I've been craving certain foods. My friends says it's all in my head. These cravings are normal, right?

Yes, they are normal as long as they are not too weird (like craving the smell of Comet cleanser or gasoline). Taste and food preferences normally change somewhat during pregnancy.

Shortly after I became pregnant, I developed a strong craving for a particular type of clay. Will it hurt my baby if I sometimes eat it?

It may. Some women find the smell and taste of a specific type of clay irresistible in pregnancy. Other women are attracted to dry laundry starch, dirt, or other substances that are not thought of as food. Consumption of clay or dirt may clog up the intestines or cause infection or parasitic infestation of the intestinal tract. If the clay or dirt settles the stomach, there are medicines that can be more safely used. Some women find dried powdered milk is a good substitute for dry laundry starch.

I've been craving ice cubes and ice chips lately and can't seem to stop crunching on them. What's up?

You may have iron deficiency anemia. Have your health-care provider check for it. Ice eating is often, but not always, associated with iron deficiency anemia. It's not known why the two conditions occur together.

Will the baby let me know when it's time to eat?

No. Your body sets off the hunger alarm.

Will it hurt the baby if I don't eat the foods I'm craving?

Food cravings during pregnancy do not appear to be based on the needs of the fetus. Consequently, you shouldn't feel compelled to eat the specific foods you crave.

Diet and Changes in a Woman's Body

My hemoglobin has dropped two points over the last two months. Is that normal?

A drop in hemoglobin during pregnancy is normal—if it doesn't drop too far. A drop in hemoglobin is generally considered to be a good sign because it indicates that the volume of blood in your circulatory system is increasing. A healthy increase in blood volume is associated with good rates of fetal growth.

Women are not considered to have iron deficiency anemia until their hemoglobin drops below 10.5 g/dl (grams per deciliter) in the second trimester or below 11.0 g/dl in the third trimester. Hemoglobins that don't fall a bit, or that are high, are more of a cause for concern than are hemoglobins that drop somewhat. A rising hemoglobin, unless it is in response to iron supplements taken for anemia, may indicate that blood volume is not expanding appropriately.

I'm seven months pregnant and had my blood tested for cholesterol and triglycerides at a health fair. I couldn't believe how high they were! Do I need to go on a special diet to lower my levels of cholesterol and triglycerides?

If you are otherwise healthy, no special diet is indicated. Cholesterol and triglycerides normally increase substantially in pregnancy, especially during the third trimester. The fetus has a high need for cholesterol, as it is required to form nervous tissue and cell membranes. Triglycerides go up because they are a source of energy for the fetus. If you are concerned, have your blood tested again after pregnancy or several months after you have weaned your baby if you breast-feed.

Fun Facts About Pregnancy

Is pregnancy really forty weeks long?

No, it's not. On average, pregnancy lasts thirty-eight weeks. Due dates are calculated from the day the last menstrual period started, and conception doesn't take place until about two weeks after that. So, the first two weeks of a forty-week pregnancy are nonpregnant.

How likely am I to deliver on my due date?

You have a one-in-twenty chance. It would make more sense to announce the estimated week of delivery rather than a date. Women having their first baby tend to deliver between forty and forty-one weeks (assuming pregnancy is forty weeks long), and experienced moms during week thirty-nine.

Will my baby be left- or right-handed?

Lifelong left- or right-handedness appears to be established between ten to twelve weeks of pregnancy when the fetus picks a thumb to suck. You may be able to get the news early during ultrasound imaging.

Fetal tissues and organs still form after the second month of pregnancy, right?

For sure, but to a lower extent. Here's an amazing example of how one tissue forms after the second month. In the third month of pregnancy, the roof of the fetus's mouth forms in just a matter of hours.

A carefully chosen diet provides the best insurance that you are getting the assortment and amount of nutrients needed for pregnancy. Nonetheless, vitamins and minerals are often taken to "supplement" the diet in pregnancy. Reasons for using supplements, and cautions about their use, are discussed in the next chapter.

~ 5 ~

Vitamin, Mineral, and Herbal Supplements

"Enough is as good as a feast."

—Mary Poppins

Two of the most powerful words in our nutrition vocabulary are *vitamins* and *minerals*. They are the health-giving, life-sustaining, disease-preventing elements of food. The general view of vitamins and minerals is so positive that we tend to believe they cannot be harmful; the more we consume the better. This view of vitamins and minerals may be the leading reason why supplements tend to be overused during pregnancy.

It has become almost expected in the United States that a health-care provider will prescribe a multivitamin and mineral supplement as soon as pregnancy is confirmed. If not, the quality of care may be questioned. The expectation of receiving such a supplement has become so ingrained that it is proving difficult to change, even though a better approach is known and recommended.

The superior way of ensuring adequate vitamin and mineral intake in pregnancy is through diet and not supplements. There are several reasons for this. First, not all of the nutrients needed for optimal fetal development and growth are available in supplements. Foods contain many substances in addition to vitamins and minerals that promote development, growth, and health. Vitamin and mineral supplements should also not be viewed as insurance against harms caused by poor diets. They are bandages that may temporarily help heal wounds caused by a poor selection of foods, but any benefits last only as long as the supplements do. Good nutrition should be for life and not just for the period of pregnancy.

A final reason caution is called for regarding the use of vitamin and mineral supplements in pregnancy is that too much of a good thing can be harmful. Vitamins and minerals, like all essential nutrients, may be beneficial or detrimental depending on the dose. For each essential nutrient, a range of intake corresponds to beneficial effects of that nutrient in both mother and baby. When intakes are below that level, the mother's health and that of the fetus falters. Health, growth, and development of the fetus are impaired when intakes of vitamins and minerals exceed beneficial levels. It is very difficult to consume harmful levels of vitamins or minerals from food. Overdoses of vitamins and minerals are almost entirely due to the overuse of supplements.

These concerns provide the basis for the recommendation that a multivitamin and mineral supplement be prescribed like any other treatment: on an "as indicated" basis.

Who Should Take a Multivitamin and Mineral Supplement?

A multivitamin and mineral supplement is indicated for women who:

• **Consume an inadequate level of vitamins and minerals in their diet.** Poor-quality diets that, for whatever reason, cannot be improved are a leading indication for vitamin and mineral supplementation during pregnancy. Nutrients most likely to be lacking in the diet are folic acid; vitamins B_6, A, E, and D; the minerals iron, magnesium, zinc, and calcium; and EPA and DHA. Changing food choices to bring diets in line with recommendations is the best path to follow. When that can't be done, a multivitamin and mineral supplement providing the missing nutrients is indicated.

• **Are expecting two or more babies.** Nutrient need is higher among women having more than one baby. The extent of the increased need is not known, but it is generally recommended that women bearing twins, triplets, or more take a prenatal vitamin and mineral supplement daily. (See "Vitamin and Mineral Supplements for Twin Pregnancy" later in this chapter.)

• **Have certain illnesses or take medications that interfere with nutrient utilization by the body.** Recommendations for vitamin and mineral supplementation during pregnancy can be based on an increased need for nutrients due to a health condition or medication. For example, gastric bypass surgery dramatically increases a person's need for vitamin and mineral supplementation, smoking increases the need for vitamins C and E, and medications used to treat seizure disorders may increase the need for folic acid. Certain inherited conditions, such as an increased requirement for folic acid or a decreased need for iron, can determine which types and amounts of nutrients should be supplemented.

If you are healthy, have carefully assessed your diet, and have an adequate intake of all vitamins and minerals and EPA and DHA, you probably do not need a prenatal supplement. If iron deficiency is detected sometime during pregnancy, you will need an iron supplement.

Checking Out Prenatal Vitamin and Mineral Supplements

There are many types of prenatal vitamin and mineral supplements available, and their formulations vary considerably. (There are no scientifically developed standards for prenatal supplement formulation.) Some will contain 27 mg of iron and some 60 mg; others will exclude vitamin D but include iodine. If you've been given a prescription for a prenatal vitamin and mineral supplement, it will contain 1 mg or more folic acid. Doses of folic acid of 1 mg or more must be prescribed. Some over-the-counter prenatal supplements are very similar in composition to prescribed supplements, except that they will contain less than 1 mg folic acid.

Prenatal supplements don't just come in pills. They can now be purchased as fortified bars, liquids, and chewable capsules. These types of prenatal supplements should be evaluated the same way you would evaluate the pills.

If it is determined that you may benefit from supplementation due to an inadequate diet, check out the supplement prescribed or others you may consider taking. Does the prenatal vitamin and mineral supplement contain the nutrients your diet lacks? Does it provide appropriate amounts of these nutrients, or around the recommended levels of intake for pregnancy? Select the supplement that does.

Supplement and food product labels list the amount of each nutrient contained in a dose (or serving) and the "% Daily Value" (DV) of that amount. The DV is supposed to approximate your daily nutrient need. Unfortunately, the DVs used to label supplements and foods do not apply to pregnant women. Some of the values are way off. For example, the DVs for vitamins A and D are twice as high and the DV for folate is 33 percent lower than the recommended intake levels of these nutrients during pregnancy. The bottom line is that you can't tell if the supplement will meet your needs unless you compare its nutrient composition to levels of nutrient intake recommended for pregnant women.

Table 5.1 contains the information you need to evaluate the composition of prenatal supplements, whether they are in the form of a pill, bar, or liquid. It lists recommended nutrient intake levels for pregnancy and the percentage of the Daily Value these amounts represent. So, for example, the recommended intake level for vitamin A during pregnancy is 2,500 IU and the Daily Value is 5,000 IU. A supplement labeled as containing 50 percent Daily Value for vitamin A would match the recommended intake level. Daily Values listed on supplement labels should approximate the Daily Values shown in the last column of Table 5.1.

Iron Supplements

Health-care providers and experts are questioning the common clinical practice of giving all pregnant women extra iron. There is concern that too much iron is being given to women who begin pregnancy with a good level of iron stores and continue to consume sufficient amounts of iron. These women in particular may develop heartburn, gas, cramps, and either diarrhea or constipation from excessive levels of supplemental iron. Women who do not need sup-

**TABLE 5.1   RECOMMENDED NUTRIENT INTAKE LEVELS VERSUS
PERCENT DAILY VALUES LISTED ON PRENATAL SUPPLEMENT
AND FOOD LABELS**

Nutrient	Daily Value	Recommended Intake Level for Pregnancy	Percent Daily Value That Equals Recommended Intake Level for Pregnancy
Vitamin A	5,000 IU	2,500 IU	50
Vitamin C	60 mg	85 mg	142
Vitamin D	400 IU	200 IU	50
Vitamin E	30 IU	10 IU	33
Vitamin K	80 mcg	90 mcg	113
Thiamin	1.5 mg	1.4 mg	93
Riboflavin	1.7 mg	1.4 mg	82
Niacin	20 mg	18 mg	90
Vitamin B_6	2 mg	1.9 mg	95
Folate	400 mcg	600 mcg	150
Vitamin B_{12}	6 mcg	2.6 mcg	43
Biotin	300 mcg	30 mcg	10
Pantothenic acid	10 mg	6 mg	60
Iron	18 mg	27 mg	150
Iodine	150 mcg	220 mcg	147
Zinc	15 mg	11 mg	73
Magnesium	400 mg	350 mg	88
Selenium	70 mcg	60 mcg	86
Molybdenum	75 mcg	50 mcg	67
Manganese	2 mg	2 mg	100
Copper	2 mg	1 mg	50
Chromium	120 mcg	30 mcg	25
Calcium	1,000 mg	1,000 mg	100
EPA + DHA	300 mg	–	–

Sources: Dietary Reference Intakes, Institute of Medicine, National Academies of Science, 1998–2002; Simopoulos, A. P., Leaf, A., and Salem, N., Jr. "Workshop on the essentiality of and recommended dietary intakes for omega-6 and omega-3 fatty acids." *Nutrition Today* 35:166–68, 2000.

plemental iron but take it absorb only a small amount of the total iron in the supplement. This leaves a good deal of free iron in the gut, which can irritate and inflame the lining of the intestines. Women who need iron are less likely to experience side effects from iron supplementation.

If you are experiencing side effects from iron supplements, you may want to check the dose. If it is over 30 to 45 mg per day, that may be the reason. If you need the iron but are experiencing side effects from the pills, try taking the iron at bedtime or with a glass of orange or grapefruit juice.

Iron pills and vitamin and mineral supplements may look like candy to curious toddlers. Because they can cause overdose reactions, iron pills and supplements should not be left in a place where they can be sampled by young children.

Herbal Supplements

Herbal supplements and remedies act like drugs and have side effects, but they are not regulated like drugs. In fact, few regulations apply to herbs. Manufacturers do not have to prove that they can be safely used by pregnant women—and don't even have to test them for effectiveness. Uncertainty about the safety of herb use in pregnancy has lead the Food and Drug Administration to advise manufacturers not to make health claims related to pregnancy on the labels of herbal products.

About one third of available herbal products are known not to be safe for pregnant women and their fetuses. Some of these herbs have been used for centuries and are considered to be safe by some people on that basis. As a hard rule, herbs cannot be considered safe based on traditional use. Some of these herbs have been found to cause malformations when administered to pregnant animals. Table 5.2 lists some of the most popular herbs that are in this category.

The list of herbs known or thought to be safe for use in pregnancy is far shorter because appropriate tests on pregnant women have not been done. Peppermint tea and ginger root taken for nausea appear to be safe.

Based on studies with nonpregnant individuals, it is clear that some herbs may cause problems. Herbs such as tonka beans, melilot, and sweet woodruff contain natural coumarins that thin the blood and may lead to delayed blood clotting. Chamomile, mandrake, pennyroyal oil, sassafras, snakeroot, and Devil's clawroot can also have quite powerful effects on the body and should be avoided during pregnancy.

TABLE 5.2   HERBS *NOT* RECOMMENDED FOR PREGNANT WOMEN

Aloe vera	Ginseng
Anise	Juniper
Black cohosh	Kava
Black haw	Licorice
Blue cohosh	Mandrake
Borage	Melilot
Buckhorn	Pennyroyal oil
Chamomile	Raspberry leaf
Cotton root	Sassafras
Dandelion leaf	Saw palmetto
Devil's claw root	Senna
Ergot	Snake root
Feverfew	Sweet woodruff
Ginkgo	Tonka beans

Vitamin and Mineral Supplements for Twin Pregnancy

It is more important that women pregnant with twins eat a good diet and gain weight appropriately than it is to take large amounts of supplements. However, a prenatal vitamin and mineral supplement is recommended for all women expecting twins or more. Iron supplements will likely be needed for the prevention of iron deficiency anemia. Higher levels of iron or other vitamins and minerals should be taken if a particular need for the nutrients is identified.

Women with multifetal pregnancies have an exaggerated need for EPA and DHA. Although a specific level of intake has not been identified, it is likely to be over the 300 mg per day recommended for women expecting one baby. Sources of EPA and DHA are listed in Table 4.1.

Questions About Vitamin and Mineral Supplements in Pregnancy

Do I have to take the supplements I was given?

It depends on the reason you were given the supplement. If it was given to treat or prevent a specific problem, then yes. If it was given to you and every other pregnant woman seen without a particular reason, then maybe not. Many health-care providers dispense supplements to all pregnant women because it's traditional to do so or because they think patients expect it. If you are unsure whether you need to take the supplement provided, ask your health-care practitioner if there is a specific reason you need it.

Are calcium supplements a good substitute for milk?

Milk is better than a calcium supplement because it contains more nutrients. If you need to take calcium pills, make sure you are also getting vitamin D from the sun (fifteen minutes of direct sun exposure on your arms, hands, and legs twice per week, discussed in Chapter 4), or are consuming foods fortified with vitamin D_3, or are taking about 200 IU vitamin D in a supplement along with the calcium. You need the vitamin D to utilize the calcium.

I find pills hard to swallow. Can you get supplements in other forms?

There may be a liquid, chewable, or fortified bar form of the vitamin and mineral supplement you're taking or need. You can split or crush up many types of supplements and swallow the pieces or mix them with food or juice. Inform your health-care provider if you have problems with swallowing. Many people swallow just fine but have trouble getting down large pills.

Should I talk with my health-care professional about herbal supplements I am taking or want to take?

Yes! She or he will want to make sure they are safe.

⤚ 6 ⤜

Gaining the Right Amount of Weight

"Am I having a baby or a little elephant?"

—Anonymous

Pregnancy has many wonderful moments, but stepping on a scale during prenatal visits usually isn't one of them. Even though pregnant women are supposed to gain weight, cultural biases against weight gain often extend to pregnant women. Concerns about gaining weight can lead health-care providers and women to unduly restrict it. Weight is such a loaded subject in our culture that the progress of weight gain is usually closely monitored and managed in pregnancy. But this is not the case in cultures where less importance is placed on women's weight. Without the preoccupation of maintaining a thin appearance, women are free to follow the body's hunger and fullness cues. In this situation, women tend to gain an average of thirty-two pounds during pregnancy. Weight gain during pregnancy in such cultures is usually not intensely scrutinized because women do fine on their own. However, this approach doesn't work as well for many women in highly weight-conscious societies such as ours because food intake may be driven by factors other than the body's hunger and fullness signals.

If inborn systems for regulating food intake have been overridden by other motivations for eating or not eating, then it may be necessary to pay close attention to the progress of weight gain in pregnancy. The potential benefits to fetal development and growth and to the baby's future health make it worthwhile to make sure the right amount of weight is gained during pregnancy.

The Right Amount of Weight to Gain During Pregnancy

The most recent standards for pregnancy weight gain come from the Institute of Medicine of the National Academy of Sciences. Although similar reports have been issued in the past, these were the first recommendations based primarily on weight gains associated with optimal-birth-weight infants. Birth weight is a primary indicator of infant health and is strongly influenced by weight gain during pregnancy. Because the amount of weight gain associated with optimal-birth-weight infants varies according to the mother's weight prior to pregnancy, separate recommendations are given for women who enter pregnancy underweight, normal weight, overweight, or obese. Table 6.1 shows these recommendations. (Prepregnancy weight status is given in ranges of body mass index (BMI) in the table. You can look up your BMI in Table 1.1.) Recommended weight gains for women expecting twins or triplets are also shown in this table. Weight gains should result from the consumption of a healthful diet.

Gaining the recommended amount of weight does not guarantee the delivery of healthy infants of a particular size, but it does improve the chances of a good outcome. Women who gain the suggested amounts of weight are more likely to deliver infants with

TABLE 6.1   RECOMMENDED WEIGHT GAIN IN PREGNANCY

Prepregnancy Weight Status	BMI	Recommended Range of Weight Gain (in Pounds)
Twin pregnancy	All BMIs	35–45
Underweight	<18	28–40
Normal weight	18.5–25	25–35
Overweight	25–30	15–25
Obese	30+	15

robust health who feed and sleep well and who do not require special health-care interventions after birth. Infants born to women who gain little weight are more likely to be preterm (born before thirty-seven weeks of gestation), to be small, and to require special care after delivery. They may also be at higher risk for developing obesity, diabetes, heart disease, and hypertension later in life.

Pattern of Weight Gain

Figure 6.1 shows the expected pattern of weight gain by the weight-gain ranges recommended for underweight, normal weight,

FIGURE 6.1   PREGNANCY WEIGHT GAIN GRAPH

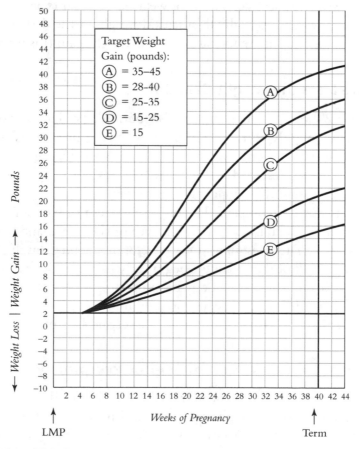

overweight, and obese women, and for the thirty-five- to forty-five-pound weight-gain range recommended for women expecting twins. Women generally don't gain any weight until four to six weeks after the last menstrual period, or *LMP* as abbreviated in Figure 6.1.

Rates of weight gain shown on the graph represent the middle of the recommended weight-gain ranges. Because ranges of total weight gain are recommended and because women tend to gain weight in spurts rather than smoothly, weight gains that are within several pounds of those indicated on the graph are considered normal. It is best if weight is not lost during any part of pregnancy, because that appears to disrupt normal fetal growth.

If you use the pregnancy weight-gain graph to chart your weight-gain progress, you should weigh yourself at approximately the same time of day while nude or wearing a similar type of clothing. Body weight normally fluctuates throughout the day, and you can get a more accurate measure of your weight gain this way.

Where Does the Weight Gain Go?

Figure 6.2 shows the approximate distribution of weight in women who gain roughly thirty-three pounds during pregnancy. Only about one third to one fourth of a woman's total weight gain in pregnancy is represented by the fetus. The rest goes to the formation of the tissues that support fetal development and growth.

Pregnancy is accompanied by major changes in a woman's body. A major increase in blood supply, growth of the uterus and breasts, and increased fat stores support the development and growth of the fetus. The bulk of these changes begin early in pregnancy while the fetus is still very small. The body becomes prepared in the first half of pregnancy to meet the exceptionally high energy and nutrient needs of the fetus that occur during the second half of pregnancy.

Weight Gain and Twin or Triplet Pregnancy

If you are expecting two or more babies, eating well and gaining the right amount of weight can make an impressive difference in your health during pregnancy as well as in the health of your babies.

FIGURE 6.2   WHERE DOES ALL THE WEIGHT GO?

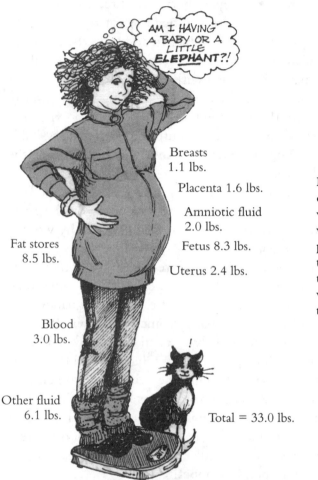

Here's where the weight goes for a woman who gains 33 pounds

Source: This illustration was developed for an educational program on nutrition and pregnancy sponsored by the Healthy Infant Outcome Project, University of Minnesota, funded by the Maternal and Child Bureau of the Public Health Service.

This section presents information that is often not covered in prenatal care but may represent the ounce of prevention that is worth well over two pounds of cure.

Dietary intake and weight gain during twin pregnancy requires special attention for several reasons. Energy and nutrient needs and stresses on the mother's body are high during twin pregnancy. Because twin pregnancies are generally two to three weeks shorter than singleton pregnancies, there is a need to eat right and gain weight as early in pregnancy as possible. In addition, the healthier women remain during pregnancy, the better prepared they will be for the hectic life that arrives along with twins.

Dietary recommendations for women expecting twins differ in only one respect from those presented earlier. Women expecting twins need higher levels of energy and nutrients in their diets. Table 6.2 presents a food group guide for selecting a diet that provides the nutrients needed by women having twins.

Individual women may need to consume fewer—or more—servings of foods within the food groups, depending on their rate of weight gain. Because of the amount of food needed by women nourishing twins, frequent snacks are in order.

Women having twins need to gain more weight than other pregnant women. In addition, relatively high rates of weight gain should begin early in pregnancy. Gaining weight early in pregnancy represents a particular challenge for many women with twins because nausea and vomiting are more likely in twin pregnancy, and they are often more severe. Guidance given in Chapter 8 on the nutritional management of this problem may be helpful for women who have a poor appetite due to nausea or who have a tough time keeping food down. It is best to gain weight when experiencing nausea and vomiting if at all possible. If your appetite is poor for other reasons, you may have to schedule regular eating times and eat "by the clock," rather than in response to appetite.

TABLE 6.2   A DIETARY INTAKE GUIDE FOR TWIN PREGNANCY

MyPyramid Guide Group	Suggested Servings per Day
Bread	8–12 ounces
Vegetables	4–6 cups
Fruits	3–5 cups
Milk	4 cups
Meat and beans	8 ounces
Oils, other (calories)	As needed for weight gain

How much weight women pregnant with twins should gain during pregnancy depends on their prepregnancy weight. Women who begin pregnancy at normal weight should gain thirty-five to forty-five pounds, or about one to one and a quarter pounds per week. (Figure 6.1 shows a pregnancy weight-gain graph for normal-weight women expecting twins.) Women coming into pregnancy with an ample supply of fat stores should gain approximately twenty-five to thirty-five pounds, or roughly three-quarters to one pound per week. If underweight prior to pregnancy, a gain of forty to fifty pounds, or about one and a quarter to one and a half pounds a week, is advised. Suggested weekly rates of weight gain are adjusted for the shorter pregnancies of women bearing twins. If pregnancy goes beyond thirty-seven weeks, weight gain, rather than a plateau in gain or weight loss, should continue up to delivery.

Women expecting triplets should gain about fifty pounds. The extra weight gain should come mainly from additional servings of basic foods.

Weight Gains That Go Off Track

Weight changes experienced in pregnancy may vary substantially from those recommended. There are several primary reasons why this happens. One is the intentional control of weight gain to keep it low. Restriction of weight gain early and late in pregnancy is particularly common among women who enter pregnancy overweight and those who are very concerned about their weight.

Nausea and vomiting comprise a second reason why weight gain may go awry. Women with nausea and vomiting in early pregnancy may find it hard to gain weight. Although it used to be thought that weight loss early in pregnancy due to nausea and vomiting was okay if the weight was gained back later, it now appears that the best situation is a continuous, gradual weight gain. For women with nausea and vomiting, it may be necessary to snack, to separate the ingestion of liquid and solid foods, and to eat foods that are well tolerated. (Specific advice for diet during nausea and vomiting is given in Chapter 8.)

A third reason for weight gains that do not follow the graph is water retention. Some women accumulate large amounts of water in addition to that needed for blood volume expansion and other purposes. An increased body content of water may be reflected in an unexpected weight gain. A high level of water accumulation can sometimes be identified by edema, the swelling of the hands, ankles, and feet. Unless accompanied by elevated blood pressure and protein in the urine, such an accumulation of water is considered normal. In fact, women who experience edema without hypertension or protein in the urine are more likely to have healthy-sized infants than are women who do not do so. The extra water that accumulates will be lost within a few days after delivery. If weight gain is due to water retention and not to an excessive intake of calories or a major reduction in physical activity level, there is no need to cut back on your food intake.

Weight gain may go off track if women consume too much food. Women who substantially lower their levels of physical activity due to bed rest, an injury, or another reason may gain more weight than expected if food intake doesn't change. If the rate of weight gain becomes too high, smaller meals and snacks are indicated.

Periods of excessively high weight gain during pregnancy should not be offset with weight loss. Rather, it is recommended that women slow down their rate of weight gain by eating less or exercising more. Weight loss in pregnancy is *never* recommended! Weight-loss programs should not be started until after delivery, nor should they be so severe as to compromise the level of breast-milk production in women who breast-feed. (Read more about this topic in Chapter 10.)

What to Expect in Weight Loss After Pregnancy

If the success of weight-loss programs is measured by the amount of weight lost, then delivery is a highly successful weight-loss program! Women generally lose fifteen pounds within a few days after delivery and approximately twenty-four pounds by six to eight weeks postpartum. On average, women who gain within the recommended ranges weigh about two pounds more twelve months after delivery than they did before, and women who gain below the recommended ranges approximately one to two pounds more a year after delivery than before pregnancy. Body weights tend to be five or more pounds higher a year after delivery among women who gain above the recommended ranges.

Weight retention after pregnancy varies a good deal among individual women. Some women begin to gain weight after delivery due to changes in eating habits or physical activity levels. Other women lose weight rather quickly. It is hard to predict how much weight an individual woman will lose after delivery. It is clear, however, that women who gain weight excessively will have more to lose after their babies are born.

A reasonable rate of weight loss in the weeks that follow delivery is one to two pounds per week. Losing weight faster may drain your energy level, make you more susceptible to illness, and reduce breast-milk volume. Be kind to yourself and don't try to lose weight too rapidly after pregnancy. With a new baby around, you will need all the energy and stamina you can muster.

Questions About Weight Gain and Pregnancy

How much should my baby weigh at birth?

Optimal birth weights based on the lowest risk of death and health problems are between 3,500 and 4,500 grams (7 pounds, 12 ounces to 9 pounds, 14 ounces). Some babies, however, are naturally smaller or larger than others and are of robust health. The chances of being optimally healthy at birth, however, are higher for infants who weigh within the optimal range. Recommended weight-gain goals are based on the delivery of infants with optimal birth weight. That doesn't always happen, though, because other factors, such as smoking during pregnancy, preterm delivery, the size of the mother, and the development of hypertension or diabetes in pregnancy, as well as other conditions, may also affect birth weight.

Should African-American women gain a different amount of weight than Caucasian women?

No, the recommendations are the same.

How much weight should I gain?

Just like panty hose, no one size fits all. How much weight you should gain in pregnancy primarily depends on your weight before conception and whether you are expecting two or more infants. Table 6.1 shows the recommended weight gains for pregnancy.

Will the amount of weight I gain affect the chances that I'll deliver early?

Weight gain in the second half of pregnancy is related to the risk of preterm delivery. Underweight and normal-weight women who gain less than 0.8 pounds per week and overweight and obese women gaining less than 0.7 pounds per week in the third trimester have a higher risk of delivering early. Low rates of weight gain in the first half of pregnancy are more closely related to the birth of small infants, especially among women who begin pregnancy underweight.

How do I know I'm gaining the right amount of weight?

First, identify your recommended range of weight gain based on your prepregnancy BMI group (Table 6.1). Then plot your weight gain on the graph in Figure 6.1. As long as you are consistently gaining some weight, don't worry if your weight differs from that shown on the graph by a few pounds.

Why should I gain thirty pounds if the baby will only weigh around eight pounds at birth?

Imagine trying to build a car without a factory. Most of the weight gained in pregnancy goes into the development of maternal tissues that support fetal development, growth, and breast-feeding. If weight gain is too low, these tissues do not fully develop or function optimally, and fetal development and growth may be compromised.

If I started pregnancy overweight, is it okay to lose weight during pregnancy?

No, it is never considered wise to lose weight during pregnancy. Women who begin pregnancy with extra fat stores do not need to gain as much weight as women who have less stored fat. However, because the fetus needs a constant supply of glucose, it is best to consume enough food to gain weight at a slow and gradual pace from four weeks of pregnancy onward.

I started pregnancy overweight and have been careful to eat a healthy diet since I found out I was pregnant. The thing is, I've been losing weight ever since I started to eat healthy. Does it matter if I lose weight if I'm eating a really good diet?

You should gain some weight. Eat more healthy foods. It is fairly common for women who are overweight to lose weight if they change to a more nutrient-dense diet during pregnancy. Although it is excellent that your food choices are healthy ones, you still need to gain weight. The fetus is more adversely affected by weight loss or fasting during pregnancy than is the mother. Weight loss in pregnancy may mean the fetus is using too much fat for energy and not enough glucose. It may also reduce the increase in maternal blood volume and compromise the delivery of nutrients and other substances needed by the fetus.

I'm gaining too much weight. How can I cut down?

Weight gain during pregnancy may occur in spurts of several pounds within a few days or a week. If this occurs because you have been very hungry and have eaten in response to this, don't worry much about short-term weight gain. Your appetite will probably decrease with time. If you are gaining too much weight and have not eaten that much, you may be retaining fluid. If weight gain is due to water, you shouldn't cut back on your food intake.

If your weight-gain pattern over several weeks to a month is too high because you are eating too much, then it's time to reduce portion sizes and perhaps to eat fewer snacks. Foods that contribute the least nutritional value should be the first ones eliminated from your diet. Increasing physical activity can also help slow your rate of gain. But remember to keep your pattern of weight gain positive.

How much weight gain is too much?

If you enter pregnancy underweight, gaining more than about forty-five pounds; if normal weight, more than forty-two to forty-four pounds; if overweight, thirty-four or more pounds; and if obese, gaining more than about twenty pounds is considered excessive. The primary problem associated with substantial weight gain in pregnancy is having to lose the excess weight after delivery.

If I gain the recommended amount of weight, how much weight will I have to lose after my baby is born?

On average, women will have about two extra pounds to lose if they gain the recommended amount of weight. Women who gain more than the recommended amount will have more weight to lose, and women who gain less tend to have only one pound to lose. Weight should be lost gradually. The weight gain occurred across nine months of pregnancy, and there is no reason to expect it all will be lost within a few weeks or months after delivery.

What problems are caused by gaining too much weight during pregnancy?

There are several possibilities:

1. You'll have more weight to lose after delivery.
2. You may have a baby who is large and must be delivered by cesarean section (although this is an uncommon reason for a C-section).
3. You may be unhappy about your weight gain.

Somewhat large weight gains in healthy pregnant women are actually associated with very few complications. The biggest concern for normal weight and underweight women is weight retention after delivery.

My partner is tall. Does that mean the baby will be big?

The father's size is only weakly related to birth weight. However, it is related to the eventual height of children.

My partner has gained more weight than I have this pregnancy. What can I do to help?

Aha! A sympathetic pregnancy! It isn't all that uncommon for partners to gain weight during pregnancy; the gain may be related to the presence of more food in the household and more eating opportunities. Perhaps your partner can plan to reduce the amount of food that will be eaten at meals and snacks. That would be a good start. Your partner should also not gauge how much is eaten based on when and how much you eat.

✑ 7 ✑

Exercising During Pregnancy

"Reading is to the mind what exercise is to the body."

—Sir Richard Steele, essayist and dramatist

Regular exercise is something that many women do not want to give up and that other women want to take up during pregnancy. Unfortunately, deciding what to do about prenatal exercise can be troublesome. Women who seek out opinions on the safety and benefits of regular exercise in pregnancy hear both enthusiastic reports of its benefits and stern warnings about its dire consequences. What is the scoop on exercise in pregnancy? Is it safe and beneficial for mother and baby, or might it be hazardous? This chapter addresses the current status of knowledge about and recommendations for exercise in pregnancy, as well as answers questions women frequently ask about this topic.

The verdict is in. Past warnings about the dangers of exercise during pregnancy are now buried under a pile of research results that show it is good for mother and developing baby. It is encouraged even for women who were couch potatoes before pregnancy. There is no evidence that moderate or vigorous exercise undertaken by healthy women consuming high-quality diets and gaining weight appropriately is harmful. The truth is that it is beneficial.

Women who exercise moderately and regularly tend to experience fewer of the normal discomforts of pregnancy, and they benefit from the sense of well-being regular exercise can bring. Regular exercise during pregnancy:

- Increases maternal blood volume and blood flow
- Reduces lower back pain
- Decreases the risk of gestational diabetes and hypertension
- Helps keep weight gain in check
- Improves stress levels
- Enhances placental and fetal growth
- Decreases postpartum depression

Excessive levels of physical activity in pregnancy can reduce fetal growth and increase the risk of preterm delivery. However, a cardinal sign that exercise level is too high is a low rate of weight gain. Exercise or physical activity that ends in exhaustion, endurance activities, and vigorous activities undertaken in hot, humid climates should be out of bounds for pregnant women. Pregnancy is not the time to achieve peak performance or fitness goals or to play sports competitively.

Some women need to consult with their health-care provider about exercising during pregnancy. This group includes women who experience vaginal spotting or bleeding, who have *placenta previa* (in which the placenta covers part or all of the opening of the uterus), who threaten to miscarry, who have a history of miscarriage, or who have what is known as a *weak cervix*.

Exercising During Pregnancy

The American College of Obstetrics and Gynecology and other groups have studied the benefits and hazards of physical activity in pregnancy and developed recommendations for exercise. The following guidelines include the dos and don'ts for exercising when you're pregnant.

The Dos

- Do exercise moderately and regularly unless otherwise advised by your health-care provider.
- Do emphasize non-weight-bearing activities and those that don't require a keen sense of balance.
- Do wear loose-fitting, lightweight clothing that allows heat to escape and moisture to evaporate.
- Do drink plenty of fluids during exercise, and eat appropriately.
- Do consume a healthy diet and gain weight as recommended.
- Do exercise at an intensity level that allows you to speak normally—as though you are having a conversation.

The Don'ts

- Don't exercise or perform physical work to exhaustion. Quit when you feel tired.
- Don't exercise while lying on your back during the second and third trimester.
- Don't exercise in hot, humid conditions.
- Don't perform activities such as push-ups or contact sports that may traumatize the abdomen or uterus or cause you to lose your balance.
- Don't exercise while you are hungry or thirsty.
- Don't exercise if it is painful or makes you feel faint, dizzy, or nauseous.

Pregnant women should exercise for at least thirty minutes four times per week. The intensity of the exercise is right if you can still talk normally while doing the exercise. Exercise sessions should begin with a five-minute warm-up period based on stretching. This is followed by roughly twenty minutes of exercise and a five- to ten-minute cool-down period. The cool-down period entails slowing the pace of the exercise and stretching.

Pregnant women can healthfully engage in a wide variety of physical activities that are low impact and that do not depend on a keen sense of balance. Such activities include:

- Swimming
- Low-impact aerobics
- Low-impact strength training
- Brisk walking or jogging
- Bicycling
- Golf
- Playing Frisbee
- Step climbing
- Dancing
- Hiking
- Gardening

Switching to non-weight-bearing exercises is advised for the last few months of pregnancy.

Exercises *not* recommended for pregnant women include:

- Skiing
- Scuba diving
- Horseback riding
- Participating in contact sports
- Surfing
- Mountain and rock climbing
- Full sit-ups
- Field hockey
- Push-ups
- Toe touches

Exercising After Pregnancy

Due to the physiological changes that occur, most women experience some level of deconditioning during pregnancy. Exercising at prepregnancy levels can get you get back into shape by about six months after delivery. Low-impact exercise can generally begin one to two weeks after a vaginal delivery and three to four weeks after a C-section. Running and other vigorous activities can follow at about six weeks postpartum. There's a pleasant side effect related to staying physically active after pregnancy. You'll likely return to your prepregnancy weight sooner than if you return to the couch.

If you experienced health complications during pregnancy or delivery, check with your health-care provider before you begin regular exercise. He or she may strongly support your plans for exercise—or have a good reason to delay them.

Questions About Exercise and Pregnancy

Can I alter my physical activity level to help manage my weight gain?

Yes. Increasing low levels or decreasing high levels of physical activity helps some women achieve the recommended weight-gain goals. Intense exercise should not be used, however, to lose weight. Weight loss is never recommended in pregnancy.

If I exercise during pregnancy, will my labor be shorter?

There is no clear answer to this question. Although it does not appear that exercise during pregnancy is related to longer labors, it is not clear that it decreases the length of labor.

I exercised little before pregnancy. Is it okay to start now that I'm pregnant?

Previous warnings about not starting an exercise program while pregnant were unduly conservative. Healthy women benefit by adding physical activity to their routines during pregnancy. If you're out of shape, start exercising slowly, building up the time you spend in physical activities as your level of fitness improves.

Is there any harm in not exercising during pregnancy?

Women who don't exercise during pregnancy may experience more of the aches and pains that can accompany pregnancy and may tire more easily than women who exercise regularly. They may also lose out on other benefits, such as a decreased risk of postpartum depression and an elevated feeling of well-being.

Exercises that I used to do all the time are more difficult now that I'm pregnant. Is that normal?

Yes, it's normal. Many women tire more easily from physical activity, especially during the first few months of pregnancy. Added blood volume, more weight, and shifting balance all contribute to making exercise harder when pregnant.

~ 8 ~

Nutritional Aids for Common Problems in Pregnancy

"This pregnancy has been full of surprises—I was expecting a baby and not morning sickness, heartburn, and leg cramps that strike like a bolt of lightning in the middle of the night!"

—Common complaint during pregnancy

It is rare that women complete pregnancy without experiencing nausea, vomiting, leg cramps, constipation, heartburn, backaches, or other common side effects. It is also rare that they aren't taken by surprise by their occurrence. The purpose of this chapter is to help you avoid these surprises and to present ways you can help relieve the discomfort they can cause.

This chapter examines six conditions of pregnancy that may be managed through nutrition:

- Nausea and vomiting
- Constipation
- Heartburn
- Iron deficiency anemia
- Gestational diabetes
- Preeclampsia

Because each of these conditions can become severe or may signal other problems, they should be monitored by your health-care provider and treated medically as needed.

Nausea and Vomiting

Why nausea or nausea with vomiting occurs during most pregnancies is one of the great mysteries of obstetrics. The presence of these symptoms appears to be related to hormonal changes and generally indicates that pregnancy is progressing well. Well, that is, for the fetus. The mother, on the other hand, may be miserable. Nausea or nausea and vomiting tend to start around two to four weeks after conception and decline gradually or end abruptly some time during the third month. For 10 to 30 percent of women, nausea or nausea and vomiting last throughout pregnancy and are only cured by delivery. Although often referred to as *morning sickness*, nausea and vomiting are not confined to the morning hours.

Nausea and vomiting that are regular and hard to stop and that cause weight loss and dehydration (signaled by fatigue, a low urine output, and dark yellow urine) are referred to as *hyperemesis gravidarum*, or *hyperemesis* for short. Women with this form of severe nausea and vomiting require close medical supervision. The goal of medical care for hyperemesis is to stop the nausea and vomiting, to remedy dehydration, and to enable women to resume food intake and weight gain. There is a light at the end of this tunnel, however. Women with hyperemesis or less severe cases of nausea and vomiting who stay well hydrated, eat a healthy diet, and gain weight appropriately frequently deliver very healthy infants.

Women with nausea and vomiting or hyperemesis are often highly sensitive to certain odors and become queasy if they smell the wrong aromas. (Just reading about the association between odors and nausea may be enough to push some women's "queasy" buttons. If that's you, skip over the rest of this paragraph.) Odors known to trigger nausea and vomiting in some women include that of fresh and old coffee, vitamin supplements, cleaning agents, perfume, aerosol room fresheners, cigarette and cigar smoke, dirty diapers, garbage, and gas and diesel fumes. Clean, cool air in an odorless environment is generally found to be soothing.

Iron supplements aggravate nausea and vomiting in many women. Generally, their use should be discontinued until women are feeling better if they contribute to nausea and vomiting later in pregnancy.

It is not known how to prevent nausea and vomiting from occurring, but there are actions women can take that may help reduce the frequency and severity of both.

• **Snack on dry foods often.** Nausea and vomiting are more likely to occur on an empty stomach, so frequent snacks may help. Dry, high-carbohydrate foods, such as crackers, vanilla wafers, dry toast, or dry cereals often go down easily and stay down. Snacking on such foods before you get out of bed in the morning may help prevent a queasy morning stomach. A wide variety of other foods have been found to help prevent nausea and vomiting. Because the best choices are different for individual women, you will be the best judge of what foods are most easily tolerated. If potato chips, hard-boiled eggs, yogurt, or canned fruits sound good to you, for example, try them. It is better to eat the foods you can keep down than to not eat enough to gain some weight.

• **Separate your intake of solids and liquids.** Eating small meals or snacks about every two hours while you are awake and drinking fluids about half an hour after solid foods may help prevent nausea and vomiting. Some beverages are better at settling the stomach than others. For some women, warm milk with a bit of sugar or pasteurized honey tastes good, while lemonade, iced tea, water, fruit juices, V-8 juice, tomato juice, sports drinks, ginger ale, or fruit-flavored sodas work for other women. Sometimes room-temperature beverages or "flat" sodas are easily tolerated. Ice chips, popsicles, or very cold beverages are preferred by some women because they help foods stay down. Because the need for water increases during bouts of vomiting, women with vomiting should drink ample amounts of beverages that are well tolerated.

• **Stay away from odors or tastes that make you queasy.** Following this recommendation may take advance planning and some help. You may need to buy prepackaged meals or have someone else do the cooking, buy gasoline at the full-service aisle (so you can avoid smelling the fumes), or give up foods that make you feel nauseous.

• **Consider other factors.** Some women find that nausea is set off by brushing their teeth shortly after they wake up. Carefully brushing your teeth later can help prevent this. In addition, nausea and vomiting can be due to causes other than pregnancy. Because it may signal other health problems, it is always a good idea to get the reason diagnosed by your health-care provider.

Nausea and vomiting persist in some women despite their best efforts to control it. For these women, medications such as pyridoxine (vitamin B_6), doxylamine, and special high-carbohydrate solutions may be given under the supervision of the health-care provider. Hospitalization may be required in severe cases of nausea and vomiting.

Constipation

Constipation is characterized by abdominal pain, difficult and infrequent bowel movements, and the passage of hard stools. Worry, anxiety, a low level of exercise, and a low-fiber diet are common causes of constipation. In rare instances, constipation is related to intestinal blockages, the excessive use of laxatives, or the use of medications that cause constipation as a side effect. Constipation in pregnancy is thought to be due to hormones that relax the intestinal muscles and to the pressure caused by the expanding uterus on the intestines. It can occur anytime, but it is most common late in pregnancy.

There are several approaches to the prevention and treatment of constipation.

• **Eat a high-fiber diet.** Consumption of 25 to 30 g per day of dietary fiber from fruits and vegetables, high-fiber breakfast cereals, bran, and powdered bulk-forming supplemental fiber such as *psyllium* or *methyl cellulose* can help prevent and relieve constipation. Table 2.3 lists food sources of fiber. It is best to check out the fiber value of foods rather than make assumptions about which ones are high in fiber. Not all foods thought of as being high in fiber actually are. Because greater consumption of fiber increases your requirement for water, you'll need to make sure you drink more fluids. You'll know you are consuming enough fiber and fluid when your stools are large and soft. Too much fiber can lead to diarrhea. Prunes, prune juice, and figs also help relieve constipation. Although they are not particularly high in fiber, prunes and figs contain other substances that speed up elimination.

• **Drink eleven to twelve cups of fluid each day.** The combination of fiber and fluids is what enhances elimination, and both are necessary. Women who sweat a lot or are exposed to hot, humid climates may need more than twelve cups of fluid each day.

• **Exercise.** Inactivity fosters constipation. Walking, swimming, or other moderate exercise helps mobilize the intestines.

• **Cut back on iron supplements.** Iron supplements cause constipation in some women, especially if the dose is high (over 30 to 45 mg per day). Constipation will often improve if the amount of supplemental iron taken is reduced or if smaller doses of iron are taken at one time.

Laxative pills are not recommended for the treatment of constipation during pregnancy because they may stimulate uterine contractions. Mineral oil is not advised, either, because it substantially reduces nutrient absorption.

Heartburn

Heartburn, or "acid indigestion," occurs when acidic fluids in the stomach spurt up into the esophagus. Although stomach juices should only go down the digestive tract, they can back up if pressure on the stomach is high or if the valve that closes the top of the stomach becomes relaxed. Both of these factors seem to play a role in the development of heartburn during pregnancy. Over 50 percent of women experience heartburn, especially late in pregnancy when the fetus exerts strong, upward pressure on the stomach. Heartburn can, however, occur during any part of pregnancy.

The symptoms of heartburn can often be alleviated by one or more of the following measures:

- **Consume small meals and snacks.** Pressure on the stomach is higher when it is full.
- **Don't eat a meal within three hours of bedtime.** Lying down with a full stomach increases the likelihood that acidic stomach fluids will escape into the esophagus. The stomach usually empties about three hours after a meal.
- **Reduce the use of iron supplements.** If iron supplements give you heartburn, the dose of iron is probably too high. If iron is needed, take a lower dose at bedtime with orange or grapefruit juice.
- **Position your body in ways that reduce heartburn.** Bending over may worsen heartburn, so try to avoid doing so. Sleeping with your head elevated may help reduce heartburn.
- **Use medications for heartburn, if necessary.** Antacids such as Tums that act in the stomach, rather than pills for heartburn, may be advised by your health-care provider.

Iron Deficiency Anemia

Iron deficiency anemia is fairly common in pregnancy and is related to preterm delivery, the birth of small infants, and postpartum depression. In women, iron deficiency generally reduces appetite, food intake, mental alertness, and productivity. It can cause irritability, fatigue, and an increased susceptibility to infection as well. Iron deficiency anemia is especially common among women who have previously experienced it, who donate blood regularly, who habitually consume a low-iron diet, who have had a previous cesarean section, or who enter pregnancy with low iron stores.

Iron deficiency anemia is usually diagnosed when blood hemoglobin levels in the first trimester are less than 11 g/dl, less than 10.5 g/dl in the second trimester, or less than 11 g/dl in the third trimester. Iron deficiency anemia is also diagnosed when ferritin levels (a measure of iron stores) are 15 ng/ml or less. Hemoglobin levels between 10.5 and 13.2 g/dl in the second and third trimester of pregnancy are considered ideal. Levels of hemoglobin normally decrease in pregnancy due to an increase in blood volume. Among women without iron deficiencies, hemoglobin levels do not increase with iron supplements.

There is a tendency among U.S. health-care providers to dispense doses of iron that are too high and cause side effects. Women with good iron stores do not absorb as much iron from supplements as do women who need the iron. Unabsorbed iron in the gut can produce nausea, heartburn, gas, cramps, diarrhea, and constipation. Stools produced when too much iron is taken are generally tarry, dark, and dense.

Rather than take excessive levels of iron and put up with the side effects, about one third of pregnant women will stop taking their iron pills. All too often, the leftover pills are put into a medicine cabinet and later found by curious toddlers. Iron overdose is the leading cause of poisoning deaths in young children in the United States. Use of excessively high amounts of iron in supplements can lead to another problem—women may not take them even if they are needed and so may develop iron deficiency later on or in the next pregnancy. How much better it would be if the proper amount of iron was given in the first place! Overloading women with iron in pregnancy is an out-of-date practice, one that is changing too slowly.

A new school of thought about the use of iron supplements by all pregnant women is emerging in the United States, and these thoughts have been implemented in much of Europe. Scientists are calling for a reexamination of the practice of giving all pregnant iron. Iron supplements should be prescribed based on each woman's need for iron. Women who have a good level of stored iron and who consume sufficient dietary iron and vitamin C–rich foods do not need iron supplements.

Gestational Diabetes

Gestational diabetes occurs in 3 to 7 percent of pregnant women, and the incidence is increasing along with obesity. It is a form of type 2 diabetes and is defined as carbohydrate intolerance first diagnosed in pregnancy. Diagnosis of gestational diabetes usually results from detection of high blood glucose levels on routine tests. Because high blood glucose levels in pregnancy impair fetal growth and may threaten fetal survival, pregnant women in many countries are given a screening test for this condition between twenty-four and twenty-eight weeks of pregnancy. If this test is positive, a three-hour oral glucose tolerance test is given. If blood glucose levels are found to be high, the diagnosis of gestational diabetes is made.

Some women are at higher risk for developing gestational diabetes than others. Women who are heavy, who have a family history of type 2 diabetes, who are older than thirty-five years, or who have previously delivered a very large infant (over ten pounds) are at higher risks than other women. Women with one or more of these risk factors will often be screened for gestational diabetes before twenty-four weeks of pregnancy.

Gestational diabetes in many women can be managed by diet and exercise. Insulin injections or other medication will be added if dietary control of blood glucose levels is not achieved within two weeks after the diagnosis. Very high blood glucose levels may be treated with insulin immediately.

The primary goal of the treatment of gestational diabetes is the delivery of a healthy baby. This is most likely to occur if blood glucose levels remain within the normal range during pregnancy.

Insulin resistance (a condition characterized by high blood levels of insulin and a reduced transfer of blood glucose into cells within the body) appears to play a major role in the development of gestational diabetes. In women with insulin resistance, normal physiological changes of pregnancy eventually lead to elevated blood glucose levels. High maternal blood glucose levels increase fetal fat deposits and interfere with normal development.

Insulin resistance lessens and blood glucose levels return to normal after delivery. These beneficial changes are often temporary, however. Close to half of women with gestational diabetes will develop type 2 diabetes within five years.

Preventing and Treating Gestational Diabetes

Getting rid of excess weight prior to pregnancy, not gaining excessive weight during pregnancy, regular physical activity, and healthful diets can substantially reduce the risk of developing gestational diabetes or can delay its onset. Maintenance of a normal body weight—along with plenty of exercise and a healthful diet—clearly decreases the risk that type 2 diabetes will develop after gestational diabetes has occurred.

The management of gestational diabetes generally involves eating a prescribed diet; monitoring food intake, blood glucose levels, and weight; exercising; and (if needed) having insulin injections. Women with gestational diabetes often attend instructional classes, and many health-care providers organize support groups for them.

Diet is the mainstay of the treatment of gestational diabetes whether women use insulin or not. To achieve good control of blood glucose levels, diets have to be individually developed (preferably by a registered dietitian with expertise in gestational diabetes) based on a woman's blood glucose level, weight, exercise habits, and food preferences. Because protein and fat in foods raise the blood glucose levels less than carbohydrates, diets prescribed for women with gestational diabetes are relatively high in protein (20 to 30 percent of calories), moderate in fat (30 to 35 percent of calories), and a bit low in carbohydrates (40 percent of calories). The number of calories prescribed and the amount of protein, fat, and carbohydrates in the diet is often modified during the course of pregnancy, depending on blood glucose control and weight gain. Some women will be given chromium supplements to help reduce insulin resistance.

Because diets for women with gestational diabetes have to be individualized and blood glucose response to the diet monitored, there is no one dietary prescription that fits all women with this disorder. There are, however, several common characteristics of recommended diets.

• **Caloric intake is set at a level that promotes adequate weight gain.** The weight-gain goals for women with gestational diabetes are the same as those for women without it. Since both weight loss and excessive weight gain can interfere with fetal growth, development, and health and can impair blood glucose control, weight gain among women with gestational diabetes should stay within the recommended range.

• **The diet provides all of the nutrients needed for pregnancy.** Diets prescribed for women with gestational diabetes contain a healthy array of foods. No special foods are required, but women should restrict their intake of sweets. Artificial sweeteners do not raise blood glucose levels and are okay to use.

• **Food intake is divided into three meals and one to three snacks.** Regular, preplanned meals and snacks are a key element in blood glucose control. Because carbohydrates in food raise blood glucose levels the most, intake of high-carbohydrate foods is spread out across the day's meals and snacks. Breakfast often contains the fewest carbohydrates. Women with gestational diabetes may be taught to "carbohydrate count" to help them plan their carbohydrate intake for the day. They may also be encouraged to consume carbohydrate foods that have a low glycemic index. These foods raise blood glucose levels less than do high glycemic index foods. The glycemic index of carbohydrate-containing foods is listed in Table 2.1.

• **The diet contains plenty of fiber (twenty-five to thirty-five grams per day).** High-fiber diets help lower blood glucose levels and control hunger better than low-fiber diets. (High-fiber foods are listed in Table 2.3.)

If insulin is necessary, dietary prescriptions will be adjusted to account for the reduced blood glucose levels that result from insulin. To keep blood glucose levels normal, it is important to remain on the prescribed diet when insulin is used. Oral medications that reduce blood glucose levels in pregnancy may be approved for use in the near future.

Exercise: An Important Component in Managing Gestational Diabetes

Exercise decreases insulin resistance, improves blood lipid levels, and lowers blood glucose levels. Walking, swimming, aerobic dancing, bicycling, and resistance exercises are a few of the options for the moderate-intensity activities recommended. Women are generally encouraged to spend thirty minutes four or more times per week exercising. Additional information about exercise in pregnancy is given in Chapter 7.

Dr. Lois Jovanovic-Peterson, an internationally known expert on gestational diabetes, offers this specific advice for working exercise into the lives of inactive women. She suggests women exercise at home while watching the news. With two large cans of tomato sauce from the cupboard, find a sturdy chair with firm back support and have a seat. Lift each can above your head with one hand five times and then lift both cans together for five times. Continue this for twenty minutes or until the sports comes on the news. (Be careful not to drop the cans when you have them over your head!) If, after twenty minutes, you are unable to sing in one breath "row, row, row your boat, gently down the stream," you have had a cardiovascular workout. If you are able to, increase the weight you lift as time goes on.

Preeclampsia

Preeclampsia is a condition unique to pregnancy and the first twenty-four hours after delivery. It occurs in about 7 percent of first pregnancies and is characterized by high blood pressure and protein in the urine. The cause of preeclampsia is not known, but it is thought to be related to insulin resistance, obesity, a kidney disorder, or chemical imbalances. Although it begins to develop very early in pregnancy, preeclampsia is usually not diagnosed until the third trimester. Hypertension, elevated hemoglobin level, increased urine protein content, nausea, stomach pain, headache, and blurred vision are signs of this disorder. Although it is difficult to predict who will develop preeclampsia, women having their first babies and underweight, poorly nourished, and heavy women are at the highest risk.

There is no cure for preeclampsia. However, women diagnosed with it may be given medications to reduce blood pressure. Healthful diets are recommended for all women with this disorder. The diet should be rich in vegetables, fruits, and whole-grain products. Carbohydrate-containing foods should be of the low glycemic index variety. Some health-care providers give women with preeclampsia 1.5 to 2.0 grams of calcium per day. Calcium supplements may effectively reduce blood pressure and appear to have few side effects. Vitamins C and E may also be given to help prevent some of the negative consequence of preeclampsia. This disorder should not be treated by restricting weight gain, caloric intake, fluids, or salt (sodium). These interventions not only don't work, but they may be harmful to both mother and fetus.

⌒ 9 ⌒

Nutrition After Pregnancy: Infant Feeding

"Food is the first enjoyment of life."

—Lin Yutang, writer

T hink of this chapter as an owner's manual on infant feeding. (The operational manual on breast-feeding follows in Chapter 10.) There is a good deal to be said about infant feeding, but with a new baby on the way or already in your life, you probably have too little time to read. Therefore, this chapter focuses on just the facts. It includes a variety of tables and lists for ready reference and highlights information that will help you make the right decisions about nourishing your infant. Answers to questions commonly asked about infant feeding are included at the end of the chapter.

Good Things to Know About Infant Feeding

All newborns, whether breast-fed or bottle-fed, have the same need for nutrients—a need that is greater than it will ever be again. Yet, fulfilling this need requires a very simple diet. Babies thrive on just one food, breast milk or infant formula, for the first four to six months of life. A baby's need for nutrients is a result of his or her rapid growth and development (see Table 9.1).

TABLE 9.1   GROWTH AND DEVELOPMENT CHARACTERISTICS FROM
BIRTH THROUGH ONE YEAR

Age	Characteristics
First days of life	Generally weighs from seven to nine pounds, length nineteen to twenty-one inches. Head is relatively large and has soft spot on top. Startles and sneezes easily. Jaw may tremble. May hiccough and spit up.
One month	Has regained weight lost after birth and more. Lifts head briefly when placed on stomach. Whole body moves when touched or lifted.
Four months	Weight nearly doubled. Has grown three to four inches. Follows objects with eyes. Reaches toward objects with both hands. Plays with fingers. Puts fingers and objects into mouth. Holds head up steadily, though back needs support. Attempts to roll over. Sleeps six to seven hours at night.
Eight months	Gains in weight and height are less rapid, appetite has decreased. Rolls over; stands up with help; sits up; hitches self along the floor. Reaches for, grasps, and examines objects with hands, eyes, and mouth. Has one or two teeth. Takes two naps a day. Loses some "baby fat" as activity increases.
Twelve months	Usually has tripled birth weight and increased length by 50 percent. Grasps and releases objects with fingers. Holds spoon but uses it poorly.

For the first two months of life, a baby will gain about an ounce a day, or a little less than a pound every two weeks. If growth proceeds on course, a baby's birth weight will triple and her or his length will increase by 50 percent before the end of the first year of life. This is an enormous rate of growth. If that pace were to continue, a five-year-old child would weigh about a ton and stand more than thirteen feet tall!

How much a baby will want to eat depends on her or his rate of growth. Babies grow in spurts, rather than at a gradual, constant pace. They will be noticeably more hungry right before a growth spurt. One very common pregrowth period occurs for most babies when they are fourteen to twenty-eight days old. So don't be shocked if your baby seems to want to eat all the time during those two weeks.

Because a baby naturally adjusts his or her appetite to the level needed for growth, you should feed your newborn whenever she or he is hungry. Feeding babies "by the clock" may lead to overeating or undereating. Wait until your baby is nine months old or more before you attempt to fit his or her meals into your family's schedule. By nine months, most babies can adjust to eating meals with the rest of the family. They will still need snacks whenever they are hungry, however.

Because babies have a great need for nutrients and small stomachs, they get hungry often. During the first few weeks, your baby will probably want to eat every two or three hours, or eight to twelve times a day. At each feeding, she or he will drink about two or three ounces of breast milk or formula. By your baby's second month, the interval between his or her demands to be fed may stretch to three or four hours. By nine months, most babies need to eat only five to seven times per day. These and other developmental considerations related to infant feeding are summarized in Table 9.2.

Feedings should be followed by burpings. Babies swallow air along with their breast milk or formula. After a meal, they receive considerable relief and comfort from a few gentle pats on the back.

Recognizing a Hungry Baby

Because babies cry or become fussy for a variety of reasons, recognizing when a baby is hungry can be difficult. Hungry babies, however, feed with enthusiasm. They shut out the rest of the world while they are eating. Hungry babies start feeding with clenched fists, suck eagerly, and forget their discomfort as soon as they start to eat. A baby who really wants something other than food will suck on the bottle or breast halfheartedly and will be easily distracted.

It is also important to recognize when a baby has had enough to eat. Accept the baby's decision that she or he is no longer hungry. Don't coax the baby into eating more or finishing the last ounce of formula or bits of food left on the plate. Healthy babies will eat when they are hungry and stop eating when they are full.

TABLE 9.2   DEVELOPMENTAL CONSIDERATIONS RELATED TO INFANT FEEDING

Age	Skills
Newborn	"Rooting reflex" present (will find nipple if placed near breast); sucks and swallows liquids; "gag reflex" (will gag if solid foods are placed near back of tongue); eats every two to three hours.
Two months	May begin to sleep longer during the night; fewer night feedings needed.
Three months	Gag reflex relaxes; enzymes needed to digest solid foods mature; kidney and digestive tract matures (baby is getting ready for solid foods).
Four months	Able to swallow nonliquid foods; eats seven to eight times per day; can hold objects between palm and fingers.
Five months	Puts things in mouth with hands; can form a bolus (a ball of food) and move it from the front to the back of the mouth and swallow it.
Six months	Chewing skills begin to develop.
Seven months	Can grasp food with fingers; able to chew and swallow lumpy foods and finger foods; sucks from a cup; can pick up cup but not able to put it down; holds own bottle.
Eight months	Feeds self from bottle (tips it up, if needed).
Nine to twelve months	Chewing and swallowing steadily improve; able to handle spoon, cup better; eats five to seven times a day.

Infant Feeding Recommendations

Recommendations for feeding infants are primarily based on energy and nutrient needs, the developmental readiness of infants for solid foods, and the prevention of food allergies. Infant feeding recommendations also include a large educational component. Many of the lessons infants learn about food and eating make an impression that lasts a lifetime. Later food habits and preferences, appetite, and food intake regulation are each influenced by early learning experiences. The following tips provide a plan for teaching your infant the right lessons about food and eating.

- Infants learn to eat a variety of healthy foods by being offered an assortment of wholesome choices. There are *no* inborn mechanisms that direct babies to select a nutritious diet.
- Infants must be allowed to eat when they are hungry and to stop eating when they are full. Infants, not parents, know when they are hungry or have had enough to eat.
- Food should be offered in a pleasant environment with positive adult attention.
- Food should not be used as a reward or punishment or as a pacifier.
- Infants or children should never be coerced into eating anything.
- Food preferences change throughout infancy. Because an infant rejects a food one time doesn't mean that she or he will not accept the food if it is offered later. Giving a food on a number of occasions often improves acceptance of it. Babies still might not like strong-flavored vegetables until they are older, however.

Feeding Infants in the First Six Months of Life

An age-appropriate schedule for the introduction of foods into infants' diets is shown in Table 9.3.

TABLE 9.3   INFANT FEEDING RECOMMENDATIONS

Age	Feeding Recommendations
Birth through four to six months	Breast-feed or give iron-fortified infant formula only.
	Continue breast- or formula-feeding through the first year of life.
	Breast-fed babies with inadequate exposure to sunshine should be given a vitamin D supplement (200 IU per day).
Four to six months	Introduce a non-allergenic cereal, such as rice cereal, and then strained, plain fruits and vegetables. Later add strained meat.
	Use iron-fortified cereal if baby is breast-fed.
	Start with small portions (1 to 2 teaspoons) and build up to larger portions (2 to 3 tablespoons) for three meals a day by six months.
Six to nine months	Use soft foods that provide some texture (for example, mashed, soupy, and lumpy foods)
	Breast-fed babies and babies given formula not diluted with fluoridated tap water should be given a fluoride supplement (0.25 mg fluoride per day).
	Give finger foods around seven months (see Table 9.4)
Nine to twelve months	Offer a variety of mashed and finely cut-up table foods from family meals.
One year	Eggs and whole cow's milk can be introduced after the first twelve months; low-fat milk should not be used until the age of two years or more.

Infants should be breast-fed or given iron-fortified infant formula for the first twelve months of life, and semisolid foods should be started between four and six months. Nonallergenic, easy-to-digest foods, such as rice cereal and strained fruits and vegetables should be introduced first. The introduction of foods most likely to cause allergic or other adverse reactions should be delayed until babies are at least six months old. Infants with a family history of food allergies, however, may benefit if these foods are not introduced until after the first year. Cow's milk, soy milk, wheat products, nuts (including peanut butter), eggs, and shellfish most commonly cause allergies. Food intolerance reactions, such as a skin rash or diarrhea, may be associated with the early introduction of corn, prune juice, orange juice, tomato juice, chocolate, and strawberries. A variety of other foods may also cause food intolerance reactions. Consult your health-care provider if you think your baby is sensitive to certain foods and are concerned health problems may arise.

Do Solid Foods Help the Baby Sleep Longer?

It was once thought that solid foods should be offered to infants within the first month or two of life. Although such young infants are unable to swallow much of the food offered (most of it ends up on their faces and bibs), or to digest completely what they do swallow, solid foods were thought to fill the baby up and help him or her sleep through the night. Giving solid foods before the age of four months does not accomplish that. Infants who are fed solids early are no more likely to sleep through the night than are those who start to eat solid foods between four and six months of age. The age at which an infant begins to sleep for six or more hours during the night depends on other factors, including the infant's developmental level and how much she or he has slept during the day. Neither the infant nor the parents are likely to get a good night's sleep for at least four months.

Feeding Infants in the Second Six Months of Life

By the time an infant is six months old, he or she is ready to chew or to gum and swallow foods with a bit of texture. Offering textured foods at this time helps the baby learn to chew and swallow and appears to foster the development of speaking skills. Foods offered should be the consistency of thick soup and contain lumpy pieces of soft food. Although you can purchase baby foods of the right consistency, you can also make them at home using a food mill or food processor.

Making Baby Foods at Home

To make baby food, all you need are a blender or a baby-food mill and a strainer. Make sure to clean all utensils, equipment, and counter surfaces thoroughly before you get started, as well as to wash your hands with soap and water.

Use basic foods that do not contain added sugar, salt, spices, margarine, butter, or other additives. After the infant is six months old, make the food a bit lumpy, but still soft.

- **Fruits.** Use clean and ripe fruits. Remove all skin, seeds, and cores (or use canned fruits). Puree in blender or food mill thoroughly. (Cook hard fruits like apples first.) Mash if fruit is soft enough. Some examples include mashed bananas; applesauce; and pureed apricots, pears, and peaches.
- **Vegetables.** Clean vegetables thoroughly. Remove stems and any tough skin or seeds. Boil or steam until soft. Puree and serve lukewarm. Possible vegetables are pureed green beans, peas, squash, carrots, and potatoes.
- **Meats.** Make sure to cook the meat thoroughly. Trim off fat, skin, and gristle. Blend or grind meat with enough water to make a puree (generally one-half cup water to one cup cooked meat). Meats you might try are pork, chicken, fish, beef, lamb, or turkey.
- **Juices.** Use frozen or bottled apple, cranberry, and grape juice. Reconstitute frozen juices according to directions on the container. Strain the juice if needed. Avoid "fruit drinks."

Freeze extra servings in a tightly covered ice-cube tray or other airtight container, or store tightly covered in the refrigerator for no more than three days. Do not thaw and refreeze.

**TABLE 9.4   GOOD AND BAD CHOICES FOR FINGER FOODS
              FOR INFANTS**

Good Choices	Bad Choices
Cracker pieces	Raisins
Melba toast (zwieback)	Seeds
Soft fruit pieces	Hard candy, jelly beans
Cheerios	Hot dog or sausage pieces
Soft pieces of vegetables	Popcorn, granola
Soft macaroni pieces	Grapes, blueberries
Small pieces of soft cheese	Nuts, peanut butter
	Raw vegetables
	Hard fruits
	Corn
	Chips
	Gum, gummy-textured candy

Make sure to discard any leftovers in the baby's dish. When the spoon used to feed the child contacts the food, bacteria is introduced that may cause the food to spoil while stored.

Finger foods should also be introduced when the baby is around seven months old. Foods offered should be easy to pick up, not require much chewing, and be in small enough pieces so that they can be easily swallowed. A list of good and bad choices for finger foods is given in Table 9.4.

By nine months of age, infants are ready for mashed and finely cut-up foods. Infants graduate to adult-type foods toward the end of the first year of life. Although most foods still need to be mashed or cut up into small pieces, one-year-olds are able to eat the same types of foods as the rest of the family. They can drink from a cup and nearly feed themselves with a spoon. Infants have come a long way in twelve months!

Do Infants Need Vitamin or Mineral Supplements?

Two situations call for the use of supplements during infancy. Breast-fed infants and infants receiving formula from a concentrate not diluted with fluoridated water need fluoride supplements after six months of age. Since breast milk contains a low amount of vitamin D, breast-fed infants not exposed regularly to sunshine should receive 5µg (200 IU) vitamin D as a daily supplement. Babies who are exposed to sunshine for a total of thirty minutes per week while in diapers only, or two hours per week if only the head is exposed, make enough vitamin D in their skin. Care should be taken to ensure the baby isn't overexposed to sunshine. Periods of direct exposure to sunshine without sunscreen should be brief—ten minutes or less at a time.

Questions About Infant Feeding

What's the best infant formula to give my baby?

Commercially available cow's milk–based formulas are recommended, and all brands are similar in composition. In fact, there are minimum standards for formula composition to which all manufacturers must adhere. It is best to use an iron-fortified formula. Babies need the extra iron to build up their iron stores. Some formulas are fortified with the omega-3 fatty acids DHA and alpha-linolenic acid. Inclusion of these fatty acids in formula appears to benefit infant vision and intellectual development.

Is bottle feeding as good as breast-feeding?

Breast-feeding is the number-one choice for infant feeding. It is not, however, best for women who do not want to breast-feed. Infant formulas are an appropriate alternative to breast-feeding for women who would feel forced into breast-feeding or for other reasons would not be able to breast-feed successfully. Although there are benefits to breast milk, the benefits don't apply if the mother is not a willing participant and breast-feeding is continued even though it is not going well.

Should I heat up the milk before I give it to my baby?

Most babies don't have a temperature preference. You may want to take the chill off a cold bottle of formula by running warm water over it. It is better to give the baby milk that is cool rather than too warm. Heating milk in the microwave can make it too hot and is not recommended.

Is it okay to put the baby to bed with a bottle at night?

The fluid that drips into the baby's mouth after she or he falls asleep promotes tooth decay and ear infections. Therefore, a baby should not be put to bed with a bottle.

Is it okay to encourage my baby to drink the last few ounces of milk in the bottle?

No. You should quit feeding the baby when she or he has lost interest in eating. If left to decide for themselves, healthy infants will stop eating when they are full. Insisting they consume more may interfere with development of their regulation of food intake.

Does my baby need vitamin supplements?

Healthy infants born at term do not need multivitamin supplements. As stated previously, some will benefit from additional fluoride or vitamin D.

Is it okay to mix rice cereal with formula in the bottle?

The practice is not recommended for healthy infants. Eating from a spoon helps develop infant feeding skills.

When can I use cow's milk instead of formula?

After the first year. Introduction of cow's milk too soon can lead to blood loss from the baby's gastrointestinal tract.

What foods are most likely to cause allergies in infants?

Many types of foods can cause adverse reactions in infants. The most common allergy-causing foods are cow's milk, soy milk, wheat products, nuts (including peanut butter), eggs, and seafood.

Do I have to sterilize the bottles and nipples?

No, just make sure they are cleaned thoroughly with soap and water and rinsed well.

How do I know if the baby is getting enough formula?

During the first month, most babies drink about three ounces of formula at each feeding, or twenty to twenty-four ounces in a twenty-four-hour period. In the second month, usual intake is twenty-six to twenty-eight ounces, and in the third month, twenty-eight to thirty-six ounces. The baby's weight gain is also a good indicator of the adequacy of food intake.

Why aren't baby foods introduced until four to six months?

The introduction of semisolid foods at four to six months is recommended because infants are not developmentally ready to swallow foods and their digestive systems are too immature to process them before that time. Introducing solids early also promotes the development of food allergies.

Is goat's milk better for the baby than cow's milk?

Goat's milk is not better than cow's milk, but neither one is recommended until after age one. Both have levels of protein and minerals that are too high for humans during the first year of life.

I've heard babies shouldn't be given honey. Is that true?

Babies should not be given unpasteurized honey because it may cause botulism in infants. Pasteurized honey is safe, but babies don't need sweets anyway.

Should I cut back on the amount of food I give my baby if he or she is getting too fat?

Probably not—unless the baby is being overfed. Babies are normally fat. They should be allowed to decide when they are hungry and when they've had enough to eat. Babies begin to thin down after they start to crawl and become more physically active.

10

Nutrition After Pregnancy: Breast-Feeding

"Mothers have as powerful influence over the welfare of future generations as all other earthly causes combined."

—John S. C. Abbot, writer

Next to every well-nourished, breast-fed baby is a well-nourished mother. She is ideally suited for making the perfect food for her infant. Breast milk provides infants with optimal nutrition and much more. It gives infants regular, oral vaccinations against common diseases of childhood, including ear infections, diarrhea, and respiratory infections. It is easier for babies to digest than formulas. Breast-fed babies are less likely to experience food allergies, diabetes, and certain types of cancer during childhood. They are also less likely to become overweight during childhood. Breast milk is the best source of nutrition for most preterm babies. Since the taste of breast milk varies with the mother's diet, breast-fed babies experience a wider variety of tastes than do formula-fed infants. In addition, the unique assortment of fatty acids in breast milk (including DHA) enhances brain development and intelligence. If breast milk were manufactured by a pharmaceutical company, it would be considered a miracle drug. Breast milk is a gift brought to us by Mother Nature that everyone can afford.

Benefits of Breast-Feeding

Breast-feeding benefits women as well as infants. When infants breast-feed, the hormone oxytocin is released and stimulates the contraction of uterine muscles. The contraction of the uterus helps stop the bleeding caused by the detachment of the placenta from the wall of the uterus. (This effect of breast-feeding can be quite noticeable. During the first few days after delivery, women can often feel the uterus contract while breast-feeding.) Breast-feeding appears to reduce the risk of developing breast and ovarian cancer later in life. The longer women breast-feed or the more infants who are breast-fed, the less likely women are to develop these disorders. An additional and important advantage of breast-feeding is that it is an enjoyable experience. Breast-feeding can be a great source of satisfaction and pleasure.

The benefits of breast-feeding for both mother and baby make it the clear choice for infant feeding. Yet, due to the demands of work shortly after delivery, a disinterest in breast-feeding, or health problems, breast-feeding may not be best for all women and infants. Women who feel that they have been coerced into breast-feeding and will never feel comfortable with it probably should not breast-feed. It may be difficult to do successfully if your heart is not in it.

If you are uncertain whether you should breast- or formula-feed, knowing more about how breast-feeding works may help you make the decision. You can also consider the following ten other reasons for breast-feeding:

1. Breast milk tastes really good.
2. One food makes a complete meal.
3. The price is right.
4. The milk container is attractive and easy to clean.
5. There's no packaging to discard.
6. There's no bottle to repeatedly pick up off the floor.
7. Breast milk is a renewable resource, and there are no leftovers.
8. The temperature of breast milk is always perfect right out of the container.
9. It takes just seconds to get a meal ready, and you don't have to go to the kitchen in the middle of the night.
10. Meals and snacks are easy to bring along on a trip or outing.

If you have decided to breast-feed, this chapter will give you information that can be used to help the experience go smoothly. It covers facts about how breast-feeding works and how you know when it's going well as well as dietary recommendations for breast-feeding women. Questions commonly asked about breast-feeding are answered at the end of the chapter.

How Breast-Feeding Works

A woman's body begins to prepare for breast-feeding during pregnancy. It does so by depositing fat in breast tissue and by expanding the network of blood vessels that infiltrate the cells of the breast. Ducts that channel milk from the milk-producing cells forward to the nipple also mature.

Hormonal changes that occur at delivery signal that milk production should begin. Because delivery—rather than length of pregnancy—initiates milk production, breast milk is available for infants born prematurely.

Milk produced by women during the first few days after delivery is different from the milk produced later. The early milk is called *colostrum* and contains a higher level of antibodies, protein, and minerals than does "mature" milk, or the milk produced when the baby is about three or four days old. Colostrum is a concentrated source of preventive medicine. It provides infants with a boost of infection-fighting antibodies for their entrance from a germ-free environment into one that is germ filled. Colostrum is thicker than mature milk and has a yellowish color.

Mature milk comes in two types: *foremilk* and *hindmilk*. Foremilk represents about a third of the available milk supply, while hindmilk makes up the rest. Present in the ducts that lead from the milk-producing cells to the nipple, foremilk is readily available to the infant. It contains less fat and protein and, therefore, fewer calories than hindmilk.

Hindmilk is stored in the milk-producing cells of the breast. Unlike foremilk, hindmilk is not automatically available to the infant. It is released by oxytocin, the same hormone that signals the uterus to contract during the first few days after delivery. Oxytocin causes the milk-producing cells to contract and thereby release the hindmilk. This process is commonly referred to as the *letdown reflex*. The milk-releasing effect of oxytocin is so powerful that milk is actually ejected from the breast. If the hindmilk is not released, the infant will not get enough milk, will be hungry most of the time, and may grow and develop poorly. A number of conditions can interfere with the release of oxytocin and, therefore, the release of hindmilk during breast-feeding. The failure of the letdown reflex is a major cause of breast-feeding failure.

Factors Affecting the Letdown Reflex

The letdown reflex can be initiated by either physical or psychological factors. It is commonly started by the physical sensation of the infant sucking at the nipple, but it can also occur when a mother hears an infant cry or even when the thought "it's time for a feeding" enters her mind. The physical or psychological stimulus signals a part of the brain to release oxytocin into the bloodstream. When it reaches its target, the milk-producing cells contract and eject their content of milk.

Certain forms of physical and psychological stimuli can prevent the letdown reflex. Stress, pain, anxiety, and other distractions can block the release of oxytocin. If a woman is in pain or if she is pressed for time, for example, the letdown reflex may not occur. When this happens often enough, women may think they don't have enough milk and may decide to switch to formula-feeding. In these cases, a lack of milk isn't the problem; the failure to experience the letdown reflex is. Breast-feeding in comfortable and relaxed surroundings, along with the uninhibited enjoyment of breast-feeding, help foster the letdown reflex.

Breast Milk Production

While an infant is consuming one meal, she or he is ordering the next. The pressure produced inside the breast by the infant's sucking and the emptying of the breast during a feeding cause the hormone prolactin to be released from special cells in the brain.

Prolactin stimulates the production of milk. The breasts will produce as much milk as the infant consumes. It generally takes about two hours for the milk-producing cells to make enough milk for the infant's next feeding. An important exception to the two-hour refill time, however, occurs when an infant is about to enter a growth spurt and eats more to prepare for it.

Infants, like children and adolescents, grow in spurts and not at a constant rate. In preparation for a growth spurt, hunger increases and the intake of breast milk may double. The first noticeable growth spurt generally occurs between fourteen and twenty-eight days of age. The increase in breast milk intake associated with a pending growth spurt lengthens the time it takes to produce a refill in milk supply. Instead of two hours, it may take twenty-four hours for breast milk production to catch up with demand. This means that for about a day, infants will want to feed often and will not have their hunger completely satisfied. Although women may spend much of their day breast-feeding an infant who is entering a growth spurt, as long as the infant is allowed to breast-feed as often as desired, production will catch up with the baby's need for milk. Adding formula to the baby's diet will decrease production because the baby will consume less breast milk.

Ensuring That the Baby Is Getting Enough Breast Milk

Unlike bottle feeding, there is no easy way for a breast-feeding woman to know how much food the baby has consumed. Breast-feeding women must make assumptions about whether a baby is getting enough to eat by signals the infant sends out. Babies who regain their birth weight by two weeks, who suck vigorously, who are hungry no more often than every two to four hours, and who are gaining weight at an appropriate rate are most likely getting enough breast milk. Unfortunately, when babies don't get enough milk over the course of days or weeks, they may not send out signals that indicate that this is happening. Young infants who fail to consume sufficient milk may become quiet, sullen, and sleep a lot. When offered the breast, they may suck weakly and not appear to be hungry. The lack of food has zapped their energy, and because they may not complain, it is hard to know anything is wrong.

If you are concerned that your baby isn't getting enough breast milk, check out the following:

- Is the baby's rate of weight gain okay?
- Are there fewer than six to eight wet diapers a day? Does the baby have fewer than three to five bowel movements daily? There should be at least this many.
- Is the inside of the baby's mouth dry? It should be moist.
- Can you hear the baby swallow milk while feeding? Swallowing noises should be audible.
- Is the baby's suck weak? It should be strong, especially at the beginning of the feeding.
- Is the duration of feeding short, or less than a few minutes? Babies usually consume 70 percent of the total milk within five minutes of beginning breast-feeding, and 90 percent by ten minutes.
- Is the frequency of feeding less than eight times a day? Babies are generally hungry eight to twelve times per day in the early months of life.
- Are you experiencing the letdown reflex? Many women can feel the letdown reflex as a prickly sensation in the nipples within the first minute of breast-feeding. You know you have experienced the letdown reflex if milk spurts, rather than drips, from your breast when the baby is removed a minute or so after breast-feeding has begun.

Not all babies displaying one or more of these signs will be consuming too little breast milk. They are warning signs, however, and should be brought to the attention of your health-care provider without delay.

Remember that breast-fed babies, like formula-fed babies, can be overfed. Overfeeding usually results from nursing the baby for the wrong reason. Babies often receive comfort from sucking on a breast when they are tired, anxious, frustrated, or simply feeling the need to suck. Try a pacifier, some cuddling, a change of diapers, or a burping before you offer your breast to a baby who you suspect is not hungry.

Weaning Babies Off Breast Milk

No one knows what the best length of breast-feeding is in terms of infant health. It has been observed over time, however, that women in most cultures generally breast-feed for six months to two years. Milk-producing animals, such as dogs, cats, mice, and rats, tend to breast-feed for about the same length of time as pregnancy. Rats, for example, take about twenty-one days to produce the litter and breast-feed their young for approximately the first twenty-one days after birth. Whether nine months is the best length of time for breast-feeding humans is debatable. However, it appears that breast-feeding for six months to a year represents an appropriate range. It is recommended that infants be exclusively breast-fed for the first four to six months of life. Any duration of breast-feeding is better than none, however.

Breast milk production will continue as long as an infant feeds at the breast. Milk production decreases when other foods are given, when the intervals between feedings lengthen, and when the breasts aren't completely emptied after feedings. It ceases altogether when the infant stops breast-feeding.

Breast-Feeding Dilemmas

Ninety-nine percent of women who want to breast-feed are physically able to do so. The psychological disposition of the mother and a supportive environment are the key factors involved in successful breast-feeding. Breast-feeding requires time, patience, understanding, and a sense of humor. It is a learning process for both mother and baby.

The greatest period of adjustment to breast-feeding generally occurs during the first seven to ten days after delivery. It is not uncommon for problems with breast-feeding to arise during this time, but with appropriate guidance and support, difficulties can usually be quickly resolved. The best way to handle problems with breast-feeding is by obtaining professional guidance and support from a knowledgeable individual. Some problems can be resolved by a phone call to your health-care provider, while others are best mended by a lactation consultant. Several resources for breast-feeding guidance and support are listed for this chapter at the back of this book. Do not hesitate to take advantage of the knowledge and skills of people who know how to fix breast-feeding difficulties.

Dietary Guidelines for Breast-Feeding Women

An adequate and balanced diet is needed by breast-feeding women for their own health and stamina, to replenish nutrient stores called upon during pregnancy, and to produce an ample supply of breast milk. For breast-feeding, you "nourish the baby by nourishing the mother."

A woman's need for calories during breast-feeding is around 25 percent higher than it is for nonpregnant women. Because energy supplied from fat stores contribute to meeting this need, not all of the extra energy has to come from the diet. In general, a diet that provides about 500 calories more per day than before pregnancy meets a woman's energy needs for breast milk production. It also allows for loss in body weight of approximately one-half pound per week.

As is the case for pregnancy, proportionately higher amounts of nutrients and calories are required for breast-feeding, and that adds up to the need for a nutrient-dense diet. The extra water that is needed for breast-feeding is generally obtained without any special effort. Women simply need to drink enough fluids to satisfy thirst.

The energy and nutrients needed to sustain the health of women who breast-feed and to produce the perfect food for infants can be obtained by consuming the variety of foods recommended in the MyPyramid Food Guide. If you are not sure whether your diet contains the appropriate assortment of foods, evaluate it as you did previously. A clean form for recording your usual diet is given in Figure 10.1.

FIGURE 10.1   USUAL DIET RECORDING FORM FOR ONE OR TWO DAYS OF FOOD INTAKE

	Day 1		Day 2	
Time of Day	What I Ate and Drank	Amount	What I Ate and Drank	Amount
Example:				
Noon	Chef's salad:		Vegetarian lasagna:	
	romaine	2 cups	pasta	1 cup
	turkey	1 ounce	tomato sauce	½ cup
	ham	1 ounce	zucchini	¼ cup
	cheese	1 ounce	cheese	1 ounce
	iced tea	1½ cups	milk	1 cup
Morning				
Midmorning				
Noon				
Afternoon				
Evening				
Late evening				

Breast-feeding women should consume enough calories to lose weight at no higher rate than one half to one pound per week. Weight loss that exceeds one and a half to two pounds per week can reduce the amount of breast milk produced. Liquid diets, high-protein diets, raw food diets, and diet pills are not recommended for breast-feeding women.

Effects of Maternal Diet on Breast Milk Composition

Milk-producing cells in the breast are supplied with the raw materials they need to manufacture milk from the mother's blood. For most substances, what ends up in the mother's blood reflects what she consumed. Consequently, the composition of breast milk varies somewhat depending on the mother's diet. For other substances such as iron, zinc, and copper, the amount that enters breast milk is regulated within the milk-producing cells and the levels remain fairly constant regardless of maternal diet.

Milk-producing cells enforce quality control processes that regulate the amount of carbohydrates, protein, fat, and many minerals in breast milk. They also regulate the amount of milk produced when maternal caloric intake is too low. Rather than dilute the energy content of milk in response to a low-calorie diet, the volume of milk decreases.

The vitamin and mineral content of breast milk can be affected by maternal diet. The amount of thiamin, vitamin C, vitamin D, and DHA in breast milk, for example, varies based on the types of foods and supplements that the mother ingests. Thiamin deficiency (beriberi), iodine deficiency, cretinism, vitamin D deficiency (rickets), and vitamin B_{12} deficiency (pernicious anemia) have been diagnosed in infants breast-fed by mothers lacking sufficient nutrient levels.

Maternal Diet and Infant Colic

The various causes of colic aren't known with certainty, which makes it a difficult problem to treat. However, certain foods in a woman's diet appear to be one of the causes of colic symptoms. Cow's milk, chocolate, onions, brussels sprouts, broccoli, cabbage, and cauliflower in the mother's diet have been related to the development of colic symptoms in infants.

Alcohol

Alcohol in a woman's diet appears in breast milk. Oddly enough, beer or wine is sometimes recommended to women to build up their breast milk supply and to "help them relax" before breast-feeding. It turns out that alcohol doesn't boost breast milk production and may slow down the flow of milk. It takes two to three hours for alcohol to clear a woman's breast milk supply after an alcohol-containing drink is consumed. A glass of wine or a beer consumed three hours before breast-feeding appears to be safe for the body. If alcohol is consumed, the amount should be limited and timed so that the baby will not end up drinking alcohol-fortified breast milk. Heavy drinking during breast-feeding can expose infants to levels of alcohol that may harm their development.

Environmental Contaminants in Breast Milk

Environmental contaminants, such as organochlorinated pesticide residues, polychlorinated biphenyls (PCBs), and mercury, are transferred into breast milk. Many environmental contaminants are fat soluble and, if consumed, will be stored in a woman's fat tissue. When her fat stores are broken down for use in breast milk, the contaminants stored in fat enter the milk. The ingestion of fish from the contaminated waters of Lake Ontario and Lake Michigan have been related to abnormally high levels of PCBs in breast milk. Other, localized outbreaks of contamination of breast milk have been reported. Clearly, women should not eat fish from contaminated waterways. Many lakes and rivers have signs posted indicating that the water is contaminated and that fish from that water should not be consumed. Your local health department can advise you on sources of contaminated water in your area. However, most often a woman's exposure to toxic substances from the environment is low enough not to harm the baby. The benefits of breast-feeding far outweigh risks associated with environmental toxin exposure for the vast majority of breast-fed infants.

Vitamin and Mineral Supplements

Vitamin and mineral supplements are not needed by healthy women who consume an adequate diet while breast-feeding. Vegans and women who do not consume a source of vitamin D or who have little direct exposure to sunshine should take a vitamin D supplement of 5 to 10 μg (200 to 400 IU) per day. Vegans should also be sure that they are getting enough vitamin B_{12} and other nutrients found primarily in animal foods.

Breast-fed babies may need a 5 μg (200 IU) vitamin D supplement daily if they receive little exposure to sunlight (less than a total of thirty minutes per week with just diapers on or two hours per week total if only the head is exposed). Infants should be prescribed a 0.25 mg fluoride supplement after six months of age.

Questions About Breast-Feeding

Should I supplement with formula if I'm concerned that my baby isn't getting enough breast milk?

Although sometimes required, it's generally not a good idea to give a breast-fed baby formula, especially during the first few weeks. Use of formula may lead to decreased production of breast milk and a dependence on formula. Allowing the baby to breast-feed on demand (which will be eight to twelve times per day in the first few months) results in a production of breast milk that matches the amount the baby needs. If your baby doesn't eat often enough, try waking him or her up and feeding every few hours. If you are concerned that your baby is not getting enough breast milk, seek the advice of your health-care provider or a lactation consultant without delay.

Some days my baby seems particularly hungry and wants to eat all the time. Does this mean I'm not making enough milk?

Your baby is probably preparing for a growth spurt. Your milk supply will catch up with the baby's need for milk within twenty-four hours. Keep feeding frequently to help build up your milk supply.

Are there foods I should avoid in my diet because they may give my baby colic?

Colic can be due to a number of causes, including components of the breast-feeding mother's diet. Eliminating the intake of cow's milk, yogurt, cheese, chocolate, onions, and cruciferous vegetables (broccoli, brussels sprouts, onions, garlic, cauliflower) may relieve the symptoms of colic in some babies. Babies usually outgrow colic by about four months of age.

Can I remain a vegetarian and breast-feed?

You bet. Make sure you're getting enough calcium, vitamin D, DHA, and vitamin B_{12} from fortified foods or supplements.

What is the best way to store breast milk?

Breast milk expressed into a sanitary container can be safely stored in the refrigerator for up to three days or in the freezer for several months.

Will I lose weight faster if I breast-feed?

Some women who breast-feed lose more weight than women who don't, but some do not. Losing or gaining weight depends on energy balance, whether you are expending more calories through breast-feeding and physical activity than you are taking in through food.

Can you breast-feed twins?

It can and has been done thousands of times. Try not to lose weight too fast, though. That may decrease your milk supply.

Will it harm my baby if I breast-feed while pregnant?

There are no studies that indicate that breast-feeding during pregnancy is harmful. Milk production appears to decrease as pregnancy progresses, however.

My breasts are small. Can I still make enough milk?

Yes. Milk production doesn't depend on breast size. Women with breasts of all sizes have the parts they need to provide sufficient milk for the baby.

Should I "force fluids" during breast-feeding?

Breast-feeding women are advised to drink to satisfy their thirst. Drinking a lot of fluids won't increase breast milk volume.

Do I need to consume 300 mg of EPA and DHA during breast-feeding?

DHA appears to be particularly important for infant development. EPA is converted by the body to DHA, so you can consume food sources of both. The amount of DHA in breast milk reflects maternal status of DHA. So, if you haven't consumed enough DHA, the baby hasn't either.

Is caffeine safe for my baby?

Caffeine does enter breast milk from the mother's diet. However, several cups of coffee a day does not appear to be harmful to the baby.

Good nutrition affects all stages of pregnancy and beyond. The next chapter gives you some delicious, healthy recipes to get you started on the path of good nutrition.

~ 11 ~

Recipes for Good Eating

One way to get the nutrients you need before, during, and after pregnancy is to prepare dishes that contain them. This chapter includes some of my favorite dishes that provide the nutrients I've written so much about in this book. Only recipes that are delicious and are rich in fiber, iron, EPA and DHA, calcium, or other nutrients of special importance to women during and after pregnancy appear here. Each recipe comes with its own nutrition information (you'll see "%" figures in the "nutrition information" sections). The figures represent the percent of the daily recommended intake level of nutrients provided by a serving of the recipes. The recipes use U.S. measurements; metric equivalents are given in Appendix B if you prefer to cook using the metric system.

Enjoy the recipes—and your nutrients.

Using a Seasoned Cast Iron Pan

No, it's not for eating. Seasoned cast iron pans are nonstick, clean up easily, help build upper-body strength (they are heavy), and share their iron with foods cooked in them. They also can last you a lifetime—if your kids don't "borrow" the pans when they get their first apartment like mine did.

1. Wash a new cast iron pan and dry it over low-medium heat to evaporate the water.
2. Using a paper towel, lightly coat the bottom and sides of the pan with vegetable oil.

3. Place the pan over medium heat until pan heats up. Then remove the pan from the heat. If you see smoke rising from the pan while you're heating it, take it off the heat quickly and let it cool down. You don't want it to get that hot.
4. When the pan has cooled a bit, add another coating of oil and reheat the pan as before. It's now ready to use.
5. After using the pan, clean it with hot water and heat it over the stove to dry. Add a thin coating of oil to the pan before each use.

Note: Cast iron pans become nonstick because they expand a tiny amount when heated and contract when cooled. Oil seeps into the pans when they are hot and becomes trapped when the pans cool.

Cooking foods in cast iron pans for ten to fifteen minutes generally increases the iron content of the foods. The amount of iron transferred will be higher the longer the food is cooked, and it is particularly high for acidic foods like tomatoes and apples.

BAKED FRITTATA

Serves 6

This quichelike dish is delicious and beautiful. It comes out of the oven with a golden brown, red-speckled top and with a crispy baked shell made from a flour tortilla. Baked frittata nutritionally qualifies for inclusion here primarily because it serves as a good source of EPA, DHA, and vegetables.

9-inch flour tortilla
2 teaspoons butter or margarine
1 tablespoon vegetable oil
1 leek bulb (white and very light green part), sliced in ¼-inch-thick rounds
½ sweet red pepper, diced (½ to ¾ cup)
½ shallot, diced
½ cup ham, diced (optional)
½ cup chopped frozen spinach, thawed and well drained
4 omega eggs

½ cup milk
⅛ teaspoon salt
⅛ teaspoon black pepper
¼ cup grated Parmesan cheese

1. Preheat oven to 350°F.
2. Coat one side of the flour tortilla with the butter or margarine. Place in an 8-inch pie tin with the buttered side down. Press the tortilla firmly against the bottom of the pie tin to shape it.
3. Bake tortilla for 8 minutes at 350°F.
4. When tortilla comes out of the oven, take a folded paper towel or dish cloth and press the tortilla flat against the bottom of the pie tin.
5. Heat oil in a cast iron pan set on medium. Add leek rounds, sweet red pepper, and shallot. Sauté until vegetables are slightly tender. Remove pan from heat.
6. Place eggs, milk, salt, pepper, and Parmesan cheese in a bowl. Mix.
7. Add ham, spinach, and sautéed vegetables to egg mixture and stir.
8. Pour egg mixture into the tortilla pie shell.
9. Bake 40 minutes at 350°F or until frittata is golden brown and egg mixture is firm. Note: Overcooking dries out this frittata.

Nutrition information per serving (⅙ frittata)—calories: 190, protein: 10 g (14%), fiber: 1.5 g (5%), iron: 1.5 mg (6%), magnesium: 85 mg (24%), vitamin A: 201 mcg (26%), vitamin E: 1.6 mg (11%), folate: 48 mcg (8%), EPA + DHA: 133 mg (44%)

BUTTERMILK PANCAKES

Serves 3

My mother taught me how to make these light and tender pancakes, and my daughter Amanda came up with the idea of making Fruit Syrup from frozen, concentrated, 100 percent fruit juice. (See Index.) The syrup tastes great and is easy to prepare. The pancakes are a good source of the nutrients in milk and folate. If you use omega eggs, you'll also get a helping of DHA.

1 cup buttermilk
1 omega egg
1 tablespoon sugar
¼ teaspoon cinnamon (optional)
1 tablespoon vegetable oil
2 tablespoons melted butter or margarine
¾ cup flour
½ teaspoon baking soda

1. Place buttermilk, egg, sugar, cinnamon, and oil in a mixing bowl and beat with a French (wire) whip until mixed.
2. Add melted butter or margarine while beating the mixture.
3. Add flour and mix until batter is smooth. Do not overbeat.
4. Mix in baking soda. Let batter sit a couple of minutes.
5. Cook pancakes in lightly oiled cast iron pan. The pan is hot enough to cook pancakes when a drop of water "dances" on the bottom of the pan.

Nutrition information per serving (two 5-inch diameter pancakes)—calories: 214, protein: 6 g (8%), calcium: 81 mg (8%), folate: 53 mcg (19%), EPA + DHA: 50 mg (17%)

BANANA OAT BRAN BREAD

Makes 2 loaves (8 slices each)

This bread is moist and tastes terrific, especially when served warm. It's a good source of fiber and provides moderate amounts of a variety of vitamins and minerals.

½ cup (1 stick) butter or margarine, softened
1 cup sugar
2 omega eggs
⅓ cup buttermilk (or add 1 teaspoon vinegar to ⅓ cup milk)
1 teaspoon baking soda
1 teaspoon salt
1 cup mashed, ripe bananas (2 medium)
1 cup flour
1 cup oat bran (or old-fashioned oatmeal)

1. Preheat oven to 350°F.
2. Lightly oil 4" × 8" bread pan.
3. Mix ingredients in the order listed in a mixing bowl. Continue mixing in flour only until it is incorporated into the batter. Overmixing at this point will cause the bread to form tunnels and dry it out.
4. Bake at 350°F for 55 minutes or until a fork stuck into the middle of the bread comes out clean.

Nutrition information per serving (1 slice, or ⅛ loaf)—calories: 168, protein: 3 g (4%), fiber: 1.4 g (5%), magnesium: 21 mg (6%), EPA + DHA: 25 mg (8%)

Oriental-Style Chicken Salad

Serves 2

Love the combination of crispy greens, toasted almonds, mandarin oranges, chicken, and oriental-style salad dressing? Use the recipe for the salad dressing if you can't find "Oriental Salad Dressing" in your grocery store. The salad ingredients include almost all of the basic food groups and provide a wide assortment of vitamins and minerals.

1 teaspoon butter or margarine
1 teaspoon vegetable oil
3 tablespoons slivered almonds
4 ounces cooked, cubed chicken (about 1 cup)
3 cups chopped salad greens (romaine, spinach, assorted wild greens, etc.)
½ cup mandarin oranges
¼ cup chow mein noodles

Oriental Salad Dressing
2 ounces (4 tablespoons) honey mustard dressing
½ teaspoon sesame seed oil
2 teaspoons mandarin orange juice from the can (optional)

1. Put butter or margarine and oil in a small frying pan over medium heat. When butter or margarine is melted, add slivered almonds and brown the almonds evenly on all sides. (This is not as easy to do as it sounds—the almonds can burn if you're not careful.)
2. Warm chicken prior to putting it in the salad if desired.
3. Place greens, almonds, mandarin oranges, chow mein noodles, chicken, and salad dressing in a salad bowl and mix.

Nutrition information per serving (2½ cups)—calories: 391, protein: 22 g (31%), fiber: 4 g (14%), iron: 1.3 mg (5%), vitamin E: 3 mg (20%), folate: 128 mcg (21%), vitamin C: 29 mg (34%), and beautiful plant phytochemicals

---

SHRIMP COCKTAIL

Serves 4

Getting at least 300 mg of EPA and DHA daily? Like shrimp cocktail? Go for it. Shrimp cocktail is low in calories, provides a rich assortment of minerals, and a bunch of EPA and DHA.

1 pound frozen cooked and deveined shrimp

Cocktail sauce
½ cup ketchup
1 teaspoon lemon juice
1 tablespoon prepared horseradish (more or less to taste)

1. Thaw and rinse shrimp.
2. Mix ketchup, lemon juice, and horseradish together in a small bowl.

Nutrition information per serving (4-ounce serving of shrimp with cocktail sauce)— calories: 114, protein: 23 g (32%), iron: 3.3 mg (12%), magnesium: 39 mg (11%), zinc: 1.8 mg (16%), EPA + DHA: 625 mg (208%)

BLACK BEANS WITH RICE SOUP

Serves 4–5

I ate this soup twice a day in Costa Rica when I lived there for a summer. It's "Tico" style, except that this recipe starts with canned rather than dried beans. The soup can include meat. (Add bite-sized chunks of cooked pork, ham, or smoked turkey to the soup while it's heating.) This tasty soup is a good source of fiber, magnesium, zinc, and antioxidants.

2 tablespoons olive oil
1 teaspoon garlic powder (or 1 to 2 cloves fresh garlic, minced)

½ teaspoon onion powder
¼ teaspoon black pepper
½ teaspoon dried, crushed red pepper (optional)
1 dried bay leaf
1 15.5-ounce can black beans (do not drain)
1 11.5-ounce can chicken or vegetable broth
2 teaspoons apple cider or wine vinegar
1 cup uncooked rice (brown or white)

1. Put olive oil into a medium-sized cast iron saucepan and add garlic and onion powders, black pepper, crushed red pepper, and bay leaf. Warm these ingredients together over low-medium heat for about a minute. (High heat may cause the garlic and onion powders to burn.)
2. Add black beans and broth to pan. Stir.
3. Bring mixture to a boil while stirring occasionally. Cover pan and turn down heat to medium. Simmer for 15 to 20 minutes. Stir occasionally while you cook the rice.
4. Cook rice according to package directions. If you want less sticky rice, place the dry rice in a sieve and rinse thoroughly with water before cooking.
5. Remove bay leaf from the soup.
6. Place a serving of the black bean soup in a bowl and top with rice. Add chopped onions and a sprinkle of vinegar to the soup if desired.

Nutrition information per serving (1 ⅓ cup serving without meat)—calories: 286, protein: 10 g (14%), fiber: 8 g (29%), iron: 3.4 mg (13%), magnesium: 91 mg (26%), calcium: 62 mg (6%), folate: 111 mcg (19%), zinc: 1.5 mg (14%), and a healthy helping of antioxidant pigments found in these colorful beans

CREAM OF (YOU NAME IT) VEGETABLE SOUP

Serves 6

Some of the best vegetables I've ever had have been in soup. Once you master the white sauce (or roux), you can use this recipe to produce all kinds of cream soups—asparagus, potato, leek, broccoli, cauliflower, squash, mushroom, green bean, celery, or spinach. Go wild. Try a combination of vegetables. You'll be getting the nutritional benefits of milk and vegetables in every bowl.

　　3 tablespoons butter or margarine
　　4 tablespoons flour
　　½ teaspoon salt
　　¼ teaspoon black pepper
　　4 cups milk
　　2 cups chopped vegetables, cooked the way you like them
　　　　best (e.g., sautéed, boiled, broiled)

1. Make the roux: melt butter or margarine in a thick-bottomed 2-quart pan. Using a French (wire) whip, blend in flour, salt, and pepper. Cook over medium heat, stirring constantly, until mixture is smooth and bubbling. Turn heat down to low and continue stirring the bubbling roux for 1 minute. Remove from heat.
2. Heat milk in microwave until it begins to steam. Gradually stir hot milk into the roux.
3. Bring mixture to boil while stirring constantly. Boil and stir the mixture for 1 minute.
4. Add cooked vegetables and continue heating the soup until the vegetables reach serving temperature.
5. Top the bowls of soup with chopped dill, chives, or a dash of cayenne pepper if desired.

Nutrition information per serving (1 cup of cream of asparagus soup)—calories: 166, protein: 7 g (10%), calcium: 165 mg (17%), folate: 99 mcg (11%)

BEANY, MEATY CHILI

Serves 9

This chili goes great with cornbread. Leave out the meat to make this a vegetarian dish. The recipe employs the Seasoned Tomato Sauce recipe (see Index) as the tomato base. You can make it as spicy as you like. With beef, this dish serves up the nutrient goodness of the tomato sauce along with a healthy portion of protein, fiber, iron, magnesium, and zinc.

1 teaspoon vegetable oil
1 pound ground chuck (or ground turkey, chicken, or pork)
4 cups Seasoned Tomato Sauce (see Index)
½ teaspoon chili powder (or more to taste)
2 beef bouillon cubes or 2 teaspoons beef bouillon powder (if ground chuck is used)
1 cup chopped onion
1 cup chopped celery
1 15-ounce cannelloni, kidney, black, or another type of bean that sounds good to you (do not drain)

1. Lightly oil bottom of a 4-quart cast iron saucepan.
2. Divide ground meat into tablespoon-sized chunks.
3. Place oiled saucepan over medium-high heat and add chunks of ground meat.
4. Cook meat until brown on the bottom, then turn the chunks over to brown on another side. Repeat this process until the chunks are browned all over. As difficult as it may be, do not turn the meat over until the underside has browned!
5. Add tomato sauce, chili powder, bouillon, onion, celery, and beans to the pan. Stir.
6. Cover pan and cook over medium heat (low boil) for 30 to 40 minutes, stirring occasionally.

Nutrition information per serving (1 cup serving, with meat)—calories: 194, protein: 16 g (22%), fiber: 5 g (18%), iron: 4 mg (15%), magnesium: 75 mg (21%), zinc: 4.6 mg (42%), vitamin E: 2.4 mg (16%), folate: 60 mcg (10%), vitamin C: 8 mg (9%), and a good-sized helping of antioxidant pigments found in tomatoes and beans

SOFT TACO WITH BLUE CHEESE

Serves 4

This is a tasty and tangy soft taco that contains a combination of ingredients you may have never imagined would wind up in a taco. You'll be holding a serving of meat, vegetables, and grains in your hands when you eat this taco.

½ pound lean ground chuck (or ground chicken or turkey)
¼ teaspoon cayenne pepper
¼ teaspoon salt (or less to taste)
¼ teaspoon black pepper
½ teaspoon onion powder
4 small flour tortillas
1½ cups shredded cabbage or coleslaw mix
¼ cup blue cheese dressing

1. Mix seasonings into ground meat.
2. Brown meat in a lightly oiled cast iron pan. Drain off fat.
3. Fill tortilla with meat and cabbage. Top with blue cheese dressing.
4. Roll it up and eat!

Nutrition information per serving (1 taco)—calories: 354, protein: 22 g (31%), iron: 2.5 mg (19%), magnesium: 65 mg (19%), zinc: 6 mg (55%)

Poached Salmon with Dill Sauce

Serves 3

As you can tell by the nutrition information given below, salmon is a great source of EPA and DHA. Buy wild salmon or salmon certified by the Marine Stewardship Council.

3 cups water
¼ teaspoon salt
½ teaspoon lemon juice
3 ¼-pound salmon steaks

Dill Sauce
½ teaspoon dried dill
¼ cup plain low-fat yogurt
¼ cup sour cream
1 teaspoon lemon juice
⅛ teaspoon salt

1. Put water, salt, and lemon juice in a medium saucepan and boil.
2. Add salmon and cover the pan. Cook at a low boil for 15 minutes or until salmon no longer looks raw (darker colored) in the middle.
3. Make dill sauce by mixing ingredients together until smooth.
4. Serve salmon with dill sauce. Note that the sauce breaks down if heated.

Nutrition information per serving (4 ounces salmon with 2 tablespoons dill sauce)—calories: 321, protein: 33 g (46%), calcium 97 mg (10%), vitamin A: 138 mcg (18%), vitamin D: 10 mcg (200%), vitamin B$_{12}$: 6.8 mcg (262%), magnesium: 44 mg (13%), EPA + DHA: 1,800 mg (600%)

CIDER PORK ROAST

Serves 5–6

Slow cooked and apple flavored, this simple recipe gives you a delightfully delicious and tender pork entrée. Consider serving it with Collard Greens and Cabbage (see Index), steamed broccoli, or coleslaw. Nutritionally speaking, it's a good source of protein and minerals.

    2 pounds lean pork roast
    Salt
    Pepper
    1 quart unsweetened apple cider (do not use apple juice)
    BBQ sauce (optional)

1. Preheat oven to 250°F.
2. Put pork into a roasting pan. Sprinkle salt and pepper to taste (cayenne pepper if you want some spice) on top of roast.
3. Pour in apple cider, and cover.
4. Bake at 250°F for 2 to 3 hours, or until interior temperature of pork reaches 160°F on a meat thermometer.
5. Top roast with warmed-up BBQ sauce if desired. Or add the sauce to the juices and serve as a gravy.

Nutrition information per serving (4 ounces pork roast)—calories: 252, protein: 32 g (45%), zinc: 2.4 mg (22%)

CRISPY BAKED EGGPLANT

Serves 4

Love eggplant? You may love this recipe. It makes a crispy, tender, delectable dish that goes great with Seasoned Tomato Sauce (see Index). It's worth all the dirty dishes it creates. And it provides EPA and DHA, protein, fiber, and folate.

    1 medium eggplant
    Salt for salting eggplant
    ½ cup flour
    ½ teaspoon salt
    ½ teaspoon black pepper
    2 omega eggs
    2 cups cornflake crumbs (or Italian seasoned bread crumbs)
    1 tablespoon garlic powder
    1 tablespoon Italian seasoning

1. Peel and slice eggplant into ¼-inch-thick rounds. Place on paper towels.
2. Generously salt both sides of the eggplant slices. Let sit for 20 minutes to an hour, then thoroughly rinse the slices with water to remove salt. Using paper towels, dry the eggplant slices.
3. Preheat oven to 400°F.
4. Mix salt and pepper into flour in a 1-quart bowl.
5. Place the eggs in a soup bowl and scramble them.
6. Put cornflake or bread crumbs in 1-quart bowl and mix in garlic powder and Italian seasoning.
7. Coat each eggplant slice first with the flour mixture (shake off any excess flour), then with the eggs, and finally with the seasoned cornflake or bread crumbs.
8. Place eggplant slices on oiled cookie sheet and bake at 400°F for 15 minutes on each side, or until the slices are golden brown.

9. If desired, top the eggplant slices with grated Parmesan, provolone, or mozzarella cheese after they come out of the oven. Serve with Seasoned Tomato Sauce.

Nutrition information per serving (¼ of recipe)—calories: 280, protein: 8 g (11%), fiber: 4 g (11%), folate: 200 mcg (33%)

BROILED ZUCCHINI WITH PARMESAN

Serves 4

This recipe is guaranteed to perk up zucchini—and your intake of vegetables. Share it with your friends who grow it.

4 small (4- to 5-inch-long) zucchini squash
2 teaspoons butter or margarine, melted
2 tablespoons grated Parmesan cheese

1. Clean zucchini. Slice each zucchini in two lengthwise.
2. Boil or steam zucchini for 2 to 3 minutes, or until it is nearly tender throughout.
3. Place zucchini on broiling pan with cut side facing up. Brush on butter or margarine, and sprinkle with Parmesan cheese. Add a dash of salt and pepper if desired.
4. Broil zucchini until top becomes golden brown.

Nutrition information per serving (two zucchini halves, approximately ¾ cup)—calories: 51, calcium: 53 mg (5%), folate: 31 mcg (5%)

COLLARD GREENS AND CABBAGE

Makes 10 servings

Talk about good for you—collards and cabbage define the concept. This dish starts with a pot full of greens and cooks down to 10 cups. You can store this dish in the refrigerator for around four days or freeze the extra for later use. Collard greens are among the most nutrient-dense vegetables there are, and cabbage is a member of the phytochemical-rich cruciferous vegetable family. My friend Coco McClain taught me how to make this delicious dish.

1 bunch (1 pound) collard greens
⅓ head cabbage
2 cups water
½ teaspoon salt
½ teaspoon dried red pepper flakes
1 cup diced smoked turkey or ham (optional)

1. Separate collard leaves from the bunch and rinse thoroughly. Rinse the cabbage.
2. Roll collard green leaves into a tight cylinder. Cut the collards crosswise into ¼-inch strips. Remove the cabbage core and cut the cabbage into ¼-inch strips.
3. Pour water into a 6-quart pot. Add salt and collards to the water. Bring the water to a boil, adjust the heat to maintain a low boil, and cover the pot. Cook for 30 minutes. Stir occasionally.
4. Add the cabbage, dried red pepper flakes, and smoked turkey or ham (if desired) and stir. Cook at a low boil, stirring occasionally, for 25 minutes or until the collards and cabbage are very tender.
5. Drain and serve with a sprinkle of vinegar if desired.

Nutrition information per serving (1 cup, with meat)—calories: 39, fiber: 2 g (7%), calcium: 79 mg (8%), vitamin A: 1237 mcg (161%), vitamin E: 3 mg (20%), folate: 63 mcg (11%), vitamin C: 19 mg (22%), and yummy phytochemicals

---

FRUIT SMOOTHIE

Serves 1

Fruit smoothies are a great get-up-and-go drink as well as a bedtime snack. You can make them using peaches, berries, bananas, applesauce, pineapple, mango, papayas—and many more types of fruit. Fruit should be ripe or soft enough to blend smoothly with the yogurt.

    1 serving fresh fruit
    ¼ cup orange juice
    ¼ cup low-fat yogurt

1. Place fruit, orange juice, and yogurt in a blender. Cover and blend until smooth.
2. Sweeten with pasteurized honey or table sugar if needed.

Nutrition information per serving (1 serving, using peach as the fruit)—calories: 143, calcium: 124 mg (12%), vitamin C: 31 mg (36%)

SNACK PACK

Makes 3½ cups

Want a healthy alternative to vending machine snacks? Here's one specially formulated to be tasty and nutrient dense.

    ½ cup nuts (your choice)
    ½ cup sunflower seeds (any type)
    ½ cup chocolate chips
    1 cup dried fruit (such as apricot, banana, papaya, pineapple, raisins)
    1 cup plain granola cereal

1. Mix ingredients together in a bowl.
2. Store snack mix in an airtight container. Carry some with you in a ziplock bag.

Nutrition information per serving (½ cup)—calories: 243, protein: 4 g (6%), fiber: 4 g (14%), iron: 1.7 mg (6%), magnesium: 57 mg (16%), zinc: 1.6 mg (15%), vitamin E: 2.7 mg (18%), folate: 101 mcg (17%)

SEASONED TOMATO SAUCE

Makes 8 cups

I didn't call this recipe spaghetti sauce because I didn't want to limit it. It's an inexpensive, all-purpose, tomato-based sauce that goes well with eggplant, beans, shrimp, and beef as well as pasta. The sauce is used in the recipes for the Crispy Baked Eggplant and the Beany, Meaty Chili (see Index). This low-calorie sauce will spruce up your intake of lycopene (the phytochemical that acts as an antioxidant and makes tomatoes red); fiber; iron; magnesium; vitamins A, E, and C; and folate.

2 tablespoons olive oil
3 small garlic cloves
1 cup chopped fresh parsley
1 teaspoon onion powder
2 teaspoons dried oregano
1 28-ounce can tomato sauce
1 28-ounce can tomato purée
2 cups V-8 juice
Salt and pepper to taste

1. Peel and slice garlic cloves.
2. Put olive oil in a 6-quart saucepan. Turn heat to medium and add garlic. Continue cooking and flipping garlic slices until

evenly browned. (Congratulations if you did not burn the garlic!)

3. Add chopped parsley leaves, onion powder, and oregano to the saucepan and mix with the oil and garlic.
4. Stir in tomato sauce, tomato purée, and the V–8 juice.
5. Cover pan, bring sauce to a boil, stir, and then reduce heat. Cook sauce at a low boil for 40 minutes or longer, stirring occasionally.

Nutrition information per serving (1 cup)—calories: 117 mg, fiber: 4 g (14%), iron: 3 mg (11%), magnesium: 54 mg (15%), vitamin A: 762 mcg (99%), vitamin E: 4.7 mg (31%), vitamin C: 49 mg (58%), folate: 111 mcg (19%), and a healthy helping of the antioxidant pigment lycopene (38 mg—that's a lot!)

FRUIT SYRUP

Makes 1 cup

This syrup is made of 100-percent fruit juice. It's a great complement to Buttermilk Pancakes (see Index).

1 11.5-ounce container frozen concentrated 100% white grape–peach juice, frozen concentrated 100% apple juice, frozen concentrated 100% grape juice, or another juice

1. Thaw juice and pour in saucepan. Bring juice to a boil in the uncovered pan and turn heat down.
2. Cook at a low boil for 3 minutes to thicken.

Nutrition information per serving (⅓ cup, using grape juice)—221 calories

---

Hot Fudge Sauce

Makes 1 cup

This sauce is a good alternative to the fudge sauces available at grocery stores. It makes a good dip for fresh fruit pieces and stores well in an airtight container in the refrigerator. It hardens like fudge when it gets cold and can be thinned by heating.

Chocolate has more than mental health benefits—it's a good source of flavanols, an important type of phytochemical for pregnant women. Be careful with the portion you serve up. This chocolate love sauce is a bit high in calories.

2 squares unsweetened baking chocolate (buy the real stuff)
2 tablespoons butter or margarine
⅛ teaspoon salt
½ cup sugar
¼ cup half-and-half
¼ teaspoon vanilla

1. Melt chocolate and butter or margarine in a small saucepan on low heat. Stir often; avoid burning the chocolate.
2. Stir in salt and sugar. Continue cooking on low to medium heat until sugar is totally dissolved and sauce is smooth.
3. Stir in the half-and-half, and heat at a low boil for 1 minute.
4. Remove pan from heat and stir in vanilla.
5. Serve warm.

Nutrition information per serving (2 tablespoons)—calories: 121, magnesium: 23 mg (7%), zinc: 0.7 mg (6%)

Appendix A

Facts About Vitamins and Minerals

A. Vitamins	Primary Functions	Consequences of Deficiency
Thiamin (vitamin B$_1$)	• Helps body release energy from carbo-hydrates ingested • Facilitates growth and maintenance of nerve and muscle tissues • Promotes normal appetite	• Fatigue, weakness • Nerve disorders, mental confusion, apathy • Impaired growth • Swelling • Heart irregularity and failure
Riboflavin (vitamin B$_2$)	• Helps body capture and use energy released from carbohydrates, proteins, and fats • Aids in cell division • Promotes growth and tissue repair • Promotes normal vision	• Reddened lips, cracks at both cor-ners of the mouth • Fatigue
Niacin (vitamin B$_3$)	• Helps body capture and use energy released from carbo-hydrates, proteins, and fats • Assists in the manu-facture of body fats • Helps maintain nor-mal nervous system functions	• Skin disorders • Nervous and mental disorders • Diarrhea, indigestion • Fatigue

Consequences of Overdose	Primary Food Sources	Highlights and Notes
• None known. High intakes of thiamin are rapidly excreted by the kidneys.	• Grains and grain products (cereal, rice, pasta, bread) • Pork and ham, liver • Milk, cheese, yogurt • Dried beans and nuts	• There is no "e" on the end of thiamin! • Deficiency rare in the United States. • Enriched grains and cereals prevent thiamin deficiency.
• None known. High doses are rapidly excreted by the kidneys.	• Milk, yogurt, cheese • Grains and grain products (cereals, rice, pasta, bread) • Liver, poultry, fish • Eggs	• Destroyed by exposure to light
• Flushing, headache, cramps, rapid heartbeat with doses above 0.5 grams per day	• Meats (all types) • Grains and grain products (cereals, rice, pasta, bread) • Dried beans and nuts • Milk, cheese, yogurt • Coffee	• Niacin has a precursor— tryptophan. Tryptophan, an amino acid, is converted to niacin by the body. Much of our niacin intake comes from tryptophan. • High doses raise HDL-cholesterol level.

	Primary Functions	Consequences of Deficiency
Vitamin B$_6$ (pyridoxine)	• Needed for reactions that build proteins and protein tissues • Assists in the conversion of tryptophan to niacin • Needed for normal red blood cell formation • Promotes normal functioning of the nervous system	• Irritability, depression • Convulsions, twitching • Muscular weakness • Dermatitis near the eyes • Anemia • Kidney stones
Folate (folacin, folic acid)	• Needed for reactions that utilize amino acids (the building blocks of protein) for protein tissue formation • Promotes the normal formation of red blood cells	• Anemia • Diarrhea • Red, sore tongue • Neural tube defects (in pregnancy), low-birth-weight infants • Increased risk of heart disease and stroke
Vitamin B$_{12}$ (cyanocobalamin)	• Helps maintain nerve tissues • Aids in reactions that build up protein tissues • Needed for normal red blood cell development	• Neurological disorders (nervousness, tingling sensations, brain degeneration) • Anemia • Fatigue

Consequences of Overdose	Primary Food Sources	Highlights and Notes
• Bone pain, loss of feeling in fingers and toes, muscular weakness, numbness, loss of balance (mimicking multiple sclerosis) • Overdose reported for doses of 100 mg or more taken for six months or longer	• Oatmeal, fortified cereals • Bananas, avocados, prunes • Chicken, liver • Dried beans • Meats (all types) • Green and leafy vegetables	• Vitamins go from B_3 to B_6 because B_4 and B_5 were found to be duplicates of vitamins already identified.
• No toxicity reported with intakes of 10 mg for up to four months • May cover up signs of vitamin B_{12} deficiency (pernicious anemia)	• Dark green, leafy vegetables • Broccoli, brussels sprouts • Oranges, bananas • Milk, cheese, yogurt • Liver • Dried beans • Fortified grain products	• Folate means "foliage." It was first discovered in leafy green vegetables. • This vitamin is easily destroyed by heat. • Folic acid is form best absorbed
• None known. Excess vitamin B_{12} is readily excreted by the kidneys or is not absorbed into the bloodstream. • Vitamin B_{12} injections may cause a temporary feeling of heightened energy.	• Animal products: beef, lamb, liver, clams, crab, fish, poultry, eggs • Milk and milk products	• Older people and vegans are at risk for vitamin B_{12} deficiency • Some people become vitamin B_{12} deficient because they are genetically unable to absorb it. • Vitamin B_{12} is found in animal products and microorganisms only.

	Primary Functions	Consequences of Deficiency
Biotin	• Needed for the body's manufacture of fats, proteins, and glycogen	• Depression, fatigue, nausea • Hair loss, dry and scaly skin • Muscular pain
Pantothenic acid (pantothenate)	• Needed for the release of energy from fat and carbohydrates	• Fatigue, sleep disturbances, impaired coordination • Vomiting, nausea
Vitamin C (ascorbic acid)	• Needed for the manufacture of collagen • Helps the body fight infections, repair wounds • Acts as an antioxidant • Enhances iron absorption	• Bleeding and bruising easily due to weakened blood vessels, cartilage, and other tissues containing collagen • Slow recovery from infections and poor wound healing • Fatigue, depression
Vitamin A 1. Retinol	• Needed for the formation and maintenance of mucous membranes, skin, bone • Needed for vision in dim light	• Increased susceptibility to infection, increased severity of infection • Impaired vision • Inability to see in dim light

Consequences of Overdose	Primary Food Sources	Highlights and Notes
• None known. Excesses are rapidly excreted.	• Grain and cereal products • Meats, dried beans, cooked eggs • Vegetables	• Deficiency is extremely rare. May be induced by the overconsumption of raw eggs.
• None known. Excesses are rapidly excreted.	• Many foods contain this vitamin, including meats, grains, vegetables, fruits, and milk.	• Deficiency is very rare.
• Intakes of 1 gram or more per day can cause nausea, cramps, and diarrhea and may increase the risk of kidney stones.	• Fruits: oranges, lemons, limes, strawberries, cantaloupe, honeydew melon, grapefruit, kiwi fruit, mango, papaya • Vegetables: broccoli, green and red peppers, collards, tomato, asparagus	• Need increases among smokers (to about 125 mg per day). • Easily destroyed by heat and air. • Deficiency may develop within three weeks of very low intake.
• Vitamin A toxicity can result from doses of 500,000 IU or long-term intake of 50,000 IU daily. Vitamin A intake from supplements should be kept below 5,000 IU per day in pregnancy. • Nausea, irritability, blurred vision • Birth defects • Liver damage • Hair loss, dry skin	• Vitamin A is found in animal products only. • Liver, butter, milk, cheese, eggs	• Symptoms of vitamin A toxicity may mimic those of brain tumors and liver disease. Vitamin A toxicity is sometimes misdiagnosed because of the similarities in symptoms. • 1 mcg Retinol = 3.3 IU Vitamin A or 12 mcg beta-carotene

	Primary Functions	Consequences of Deficiency
2. Beta-Carotene (a vitamin A precursor, or "provitamin")	• Acts as an antioxidant; prevents damage to cell membranes and the contents of cells by repairing damage caused by free radicals	• Deficiency disease related only to lack of vitamin A
Vitamin E (tocopherol)	• Acts as an antioxidant, prevents damage to cell membranes in blood cells, lungs, and other tissues by repairing damage caused by free radicals • Reduces the ability of LDL-cholesterol (the "bad" cholesterol) to form plaque in arteries	• Muscle loss, nerve damage • Anemia • Weakness
Vitamin D (125 dihydroxy-cholecalciferol)	• Needed for the absorption of calcium and phosphorus in the gut and in bones	• Weak, deformed bones (children) • Loss of calcium from bones (adults) • Inadequate vitamin D status may be common

Consequences of Overdose	Primary Food Sources	Highlights and Notes
• High supplemental doses (over 12 mg/day for months) may turn skin yellow-orange and damage lungs. • Possibly related to reversible loss of fertility in women	• Deep orange, yellow, and green vegetables and fruits, such as carrots, sweet potatoes, pumpkin, spinach, collards, red peppers, broccoli, cantaloupe, apricots, vegetable juice	• The body converts beta-carotene to vitamin A. Other carotenes are also present in food, and some are converted to vitamin A. Beta-carotene and vitamin A perform different roles in the body, however.
• Intakes of up to 400 IU per day are unrelated to toxic side effects	• Oils and fats • Salad dressings, mayonnaise, margarine, shortening, butter • Whole grains, wheat germ • Leafy, green vegetables • Nuts and seeds • Eggs	• Vitamin E is destroyed by exposure to oxygen and heat. • Oils naturally contain vitamin E. It's there to protect the fat from breakdown due to free radicals. • Supplements do not make people "sexy." • 1 mg α-tocopherol = 1.49 IU
• Mental retardation in young children • Abnormal bone growth and formation • Nausea, diarrhea, irritability, weight loss • Deposition of calcium in organs such as the kidneys, liver, and heart	• Vitamin D is present in animal and fortified products only. • Vitamin D–fortified milk and margarine • Butter • Fish • Eggs • Cheese, yogurt, and ice cream are generally not fortified with vitamin D.	• Intakes should not exceed 1,200 IU per day. • Vitamin D is manufactured from cholesterol in cells beneath the surface of the skin upon exposure to sunlight. • Recommended intake levels (in 2005) may be low.

	Primary Functions	Consequences of Deficiency
Vitamin K (phylloqui- none, menaquinone)	• Is an essential component of mechanisms that cause blood to clot when bleeding occurs • Aids in the incorporation of calcium into bones	• Bleeding, bruises • Decreased calcium in bones • Deficiency is rare. May be induced by the long-term use (months or more) of antibiotics.

B. Minerals

Calcium	• Component of bones and teeth • Needed for muscle and nerve activity, blood clotting	• Poorly mineralized, weak bones • Stunted growth in children • Convulsions, muscle spasms • Contributes to osteoporosis
Phosphorus	• Component of bones and teeth • Component of certain enzymes and other substances involved in energy formation • Needed to maintain the right acid/base balance of body fluids	• Loss of appetite • Nausea, vomiting • Weakness • Confusion • Loss of calcium from bones

Consequences of Overdose	Primary Food Sources	Highlights and Notes
• Toxicity is only a problem when synthetic forms of vitamin K are taken in excessive amounts. That may cause liver disease.	• Leafy, green vegetables • Grain products	• Vitamin K is produced by bacteria in the gut. Part of our vitamin K supply comes from these bacteria. • Newborns are given a vitamin K injection because they have "sterile" guts and consequently no vitamin K–producing bacteria.
• Drowsiness • Calcium deposits in kidney, liver, and other tissues • Suppression of bone remodeling • Safe upper intake level is 2.5 g or more calcium per day.	• Milk and milk products (cheese, yogurt) • Spinach, collard greens, broccoli • Fortified orange juice • Dried beans	• The average intake of calcium among U.S. women is 60 percent of that recommended • One in four women in the U.S. develops osteoporosis.
• Loss of calcium from bones • Muscle spasms	• Milk and milk products (cheese, yogurt) • Meats • Seeds, nuts • Phosphates added to foods	• Deficiency is generally related to disease processes.

	Primary Functions	Consequences of Deficiency
Magnesium	• Component of bones and teeth • Needed for nerve activity • Activates enzymes involved in energy and protein formation	• Stunted growth in children • Weakness • Muscle spasms • Personality changes
Iron	• Transports oxygen as a component of hemoglobin in red blood cells • Component of myoglobin (a muscle protein) • Needed for certain reactions involving energy formation	• Iron deficiency • Iron deficiency anemia • Weakness, fatigue • Pale appearance • Reduced attention span and resistance to infection
Zinc	• Required for the activation of many enzymes involved in the reproduction of proteins • Component of insulin	• Growth failure • Delayed sexual maturation • Slow wound healing • Loss of taste and appetite • In pregnancy, low–birth–weight infants and preterm delivery

Consequences of Overdose	Primary Food Sources	Highlights and Notes
• Diarrhea • Dehydration • Impaired nerve activity due to disrupted utilization of calcium	• Plant foods (dried beans, tofu, peanuts, wild rice, bean sprouts, green vegetables) • Breads and cereals • Coffee	• Magnesium is primarily found in plant foods, where it is attached to chlorophyll. • Average intake among U.S. women is marginally adequate.
• "Iron poisoning" • Hereditary hemochromatosis • Vomiting, abdominal pain • Blue coloration of skin • Shock • Heart failure • Diabetes	• Liver, beef, pork • Dried beans • Iron-fortified cereals • Prunes, apricots, raisins • Spinach	• Cooking foods, especially acidic foods like tomatoes, in iron pans dramatically increases the iron content of the foods. • Iron deficiency is the most common nutritional deficiency in the world. • Average iron intake of women in the U.S. is low. • Vitamin C increases iron absorption from plant foods.
• Over 25 mg per day is associated with nausea, vomiting, weakness, fatigue, susceptibility to infection, copper deficiency.	• Meats (all kinds) • Grains • Nuts • Milk and milk products (cheese, yogurt)	• Like iron, zinc is better absorbed from meats than from plants. • Marginal zinc deficiency may be common, especially in children.

	Primary Functions	**Consequences of Deficiency**
Iodine	• Component of thyroid hormones that help regulate energy production and growth	• Goiter • Cretinism in newborns (mental retardation, hearing loss, growth failure)
Selenium	• Acts as an antioxidant in conjunction with vitamin E (protects cells from damage due to exposure to oxygen)	• Anemia • Muscle pain and tenderness • "Keshan" disease • Heart failure

Consequences of Overdose	Primary Food Sources	Highlights and Notes
• Over 1 mg per day may produce pimples, goiter, and decreased thyroid function.	• Iodized salt • Milk and milk products • Seaweed, seafood • Bread from commercial bakeries	• Iodine deficiency was a major problem in the United States in the 1920s and 1930s. Deficiency remains a major health problem in some developing countries. • Amount of iodine in plants depends on iodine content of soil. • Much of the iodine in our diet comes from the incidental addition of iodine to foods from the compounds processors use to clean foods.
• Doses of over 2 mg per day associated with "selenosis." Symptoms of selenosis are hair and fingernail loss, weakness, liver damage, irritability, "garlic" or "metallic" breath	• Meats and seafood • Eggs • Whole grains	• Content in foods depends on amount of selenium in soil, water, and animal feeds. • May play a role in the prevention of some types of cancer

	Primary Functions	Consequences of Deficiency
Copper	• Component of enzymes involved in the body's utilization of iron, oxygen, cholesterol, and glucose	• Anemia • Seizures • Nerve and bone abnormalities in children • Growth failure
Fluoride	• Component of bones and teeth (enamel)	• Tooth decay and other dental diseases
Manganese	• Needed for the formation of body fat and bone	• Weight loss • Rash • Nausea and vomiting
Chromium	• Required for the normal utilization of glucose	• Poor blood glucose control • Weight loss
Molybdenum	• Component of enzymes involved in the transfer of oxygen from one molecule to another	• Rapid heartbeat and breathing • Nausea, vomiting • Coma

Consequences of Overdose	Primary Food Sources	Highlights and Notes
• "Wilson's" disease (excessive accumulation of copper in the liver and kidneys) • Vomiting, diarrhea • Tremors • Liver disease	• Oysters, lobster, crab • Liver • Grains • Dried beans • Nuts and seeds	• Toxicity can result from copper pipes and cooking pans. • Average intake in the United States is thought to be marginal.
• "Fluorosis" • Brittle bones • Mottled teeth • Nerve abnormalities	• Fluoridated water and foods and beverages made with it • Tea • Shrimp, crab	• Toothpastes, mouth rinses, and other dental care products may provide fluoride. • Fluoride overdose has been caused by ingestion of fluoridated toothpaste.
• Infertility in men • Disruptions in the nervous system (psychotic symptoms) • Muscle spasms	• Whole grains • Coffee, tea • Dried beans • Nuts	• Toxicity is related to overexposure to manganese dust in miners.
• Kidney and skin damage	• Whole grains • Liver, meat • Beer, wine	• Toxicity usually results from exposure in chrome-making industries.
• Loss of copper from the body • Joint pain • Growth failure • Anemia • Gout	• Dried beans • Grains • Dark green vegetables • Liver • Milk and milk products	• Deficiency is extraordinarily rare.

	Primary Functions	Consequences of Deficiency
Sodium	• Needed to maintain the right acid/base balance in body fluids • Helps maintain an appropriate amount of water in blood and body tissues • Needed for muscle and nerve activity	• Weakness • Apathy • Poor appetite • Muscle cramps • Headache • Swelling
Potassium	• Same as for sodium	• Weakness • Irritability, mental confusion • Irregular heartbeat • Paralysis
Chloride	• Component of hydrochloric acid secreted by the stomach (used in digestion) • Needed to maintain the right acid/base balance of body fluids • Helps maintain an appropriate water balance in the body	• Muscle cramps • Apathy • Poor appetite

Consequences of Overdose	Primary Food Sources	Highlights and Notes
• High blood pressure in susceptible people • Kidney disease • Heart problems	• Foods processed with salt • Cured foods (corned beef, ham, bacon, pickles, sauerkraut) • Table and sea salt	• Very few foods naturally contain much sodium. • Processed foods are the leading source of dietary sodium. • High-sodium diets are associated with the development of hypertension in "salt-sensitive" people.
• Irregular heartbeat, heart attack	• Plant foods (potatoes, squash, lima beans, plantains, bananas, oranges, avocados) • Meats • Milk and milk products • Coffee	• Content in vegetables is often reduced in processed foods. • Diuretics (water pills) and other antihypertension drugs may deplete potassium. • Salt substitutes often contain potassium.
• Vomiting	• Same as for sodium. (Most of the chloride in our diets comes from salt.)	• Excessive vomiting and diarrhea may cause chloride deficiency.

Sources: Food and Drug Administration (Department of Health and Human Services). Nutrition labeling. Federal Register, November 27, 1991. National Academy of Sciences (Institute of Medicine). Dietary Reference Intakes. Washington, DC: National Academies Press, 1997–2002.

Food Sources of Vitamins and Minerals

A. Vitamins

Vitamin A (Retinol)

Food	Vitamin A (Retinol)	
	Amount	mcg
Meats		
Liver	3 ounces	9,124
Salmon	3 ounces	53
Eggs		
Egg	1 medium	84
Milk and Milk Products		
Milk, skim, fortified	1 cup	149
Milk, 2% fat	1 cup	139
American cheese	1 ounce	82
Milk, whole	1 cup	76
Swiss cheese	1 ounce	65
Fats		
Margarine, fortified	1 teaspoon	46
Butter	1 teaspoon	38

Beta-Carotene

Food	Beta-Carotene Amount	mcg RE
Vegetables		
Pumpkin	½ cup	2,712
Sweet potato	½ cup	1,935
Carrots, raw	1 medium	1,913
Spinach, cooked	½ cup	739
Collard greens, cooked	½ cup	175
Broccoli	½ cup	109
Winter squash	½ cup	53
Green peppers	½ cup	40
Fruits		
Cantaloupe	¼ whole	430
Apricots, canned	½ cup	210
Nectarine	1	101
Watermelon	2 cups	59
Peaches, canned	½ cup	47
Papaya	½ cup	20

Vitamin D

Food	Vitamin D Amount	mcg
Milk		
Milk, whole, low-fat, or skim	1 cup	2.5
Fish and Seafood		
Salmon	3 ounces	8.5
Tuna	3 ounces	3.8
Shrimp	3 ounces	3.2
Organ Meats		
Beef liver	3 ounces	1.0
Chicken liver	3 ounces	1.0
Eggs		
Egg yolk	1	0.7

Vitamin E

Food	Vitamin E	
	Amount	**mg**
Oils		
Oil	1 tablespoon	4.5
Mayonnaise	1 tablespoon	2.3
Margarine	1 tablespoon	1.8
Salad Dressing	1 tablespoon	1.5
Nuts and Seeds		
Sunflower seeds	¼ cup	18.2
Almonds	¼ cup	8.5
Peanuts	¼ cup	3.3
Cashews	¼ cup	0.5
Vegetables		
Sweet potato	½ cup	4.6
Collard greens	½ cup	2.1
Asparagus	½ cup	1.4
Spinach, raw	1 cup	1.0
Grains		
Wheat germ	2 tablespoons	2.8
Bread, whole wheat	1 slice	1.7
Bread, white	1 slice	0.8
Seafood		
Crab	3 ounces	3.0
Shrimp	3 ounces	2.5
Fish	3 ounces	1.6

Vitamin C

Food	Vitamin C	
	Amount	mg
Fruits		
Orange juice with vitamin C	1 cup	108
Kiwi fruit	1, or ½ cup	108
Orange	1	85
Cranberry juice cocktail	¾ cup	68
Cantaloupe	¼ whole	63
Orange juice	6 ounces	62
Grapefruit juice	6 ounces	57
Grapefruit	½ whole	51
Strawberries	½ cup	48
V-8 juice	¾ cup	45
Tomato juice	¾ cup	33
Raspberries	½ cup	18
Watermelon	1 cup	15
Vegetables		
Green peppers	½ cup	95
Cauliflower, raw	½ cup	75
Broccoli	½ cup	70
Brussels sprouts	½ cup	65
Collard greens	½ cup	48
Vegetable (V-8) juice	¾ cup	45
Tomato juice	¾ cup	33
Cauliflower, cooked	½ cup	30
Potato	1	29
Tomato	½	23

Thiamin

Food	Thiamin Amount	mg
Meats		
Pork roast	3 ounces	0.8
Beef	3 ounces	0.4
Ham	3 ounces	0.4
Liver	3 ounces	0.2
Nuts and Seeds		
Sunflower seeds	¼ cup	0.7
Peanuts	¼ cup	0.1
Almonds	¼ cup	0.1
Grains		
Bran flakes	1 cup	0.6
Macaroni	1 cup	0.2
Rice	1 cup	0.2
Bread	1 slice	0.1
Vegetables		
Peas	½ cup	0.3
Lima beans	½ cup	0.2
Corn	½ cup	0.1
Broccoli	½ cup	0.1
Potato	1	0.1
Fruit		
Orange juice	1 cup	0.2
Orange	1	0.1
Avocado	½	0.1

Riboflavin

Food	Riboflavin Amount	mg
Milk and Milk Products		
Milk, whole	1 cup	0.5
Milk, low-fat	1 cup	0.5
Yogurt, low-fat	1 cup	0.5
Milk, skim	1 cup	0.4
Yogurt	1 cup	0.1
American cheese	1 ounce	0.1
Cheddar cheese	1 ounce	0.1
Meats		
Liver	3 ounces	3.6
Pork chop	3 ounces	0.3
Beef	3 ounces	0.2
Tuna	½ cup	0.1
Vegetables		
Collard greens	½ cup	0.3
Broccoli	½ cup	0.2
Spinach, cooked	½ cup	0.1
Eggs		
Egg	1	0.2
Grains		
Macaroni	1 cup	0.1
Bread	1 slice	0.1

Niacin

Food	Niacin	
	Amount	mg
Meats		
Liver	3 ounces	14.0
Tuna	½ cup	10.3
Turkey	3 ounces	9.5
Chicken	3 ounces	7.9
Salmon	3 ounces	6.9
Veal	3 ounces	5.2
Beef (round steak)	3 ounces	5.1
Pork	3 ounces	4.5
Haddock	3 ounces	2.7
Scallops	3 ounces	1.1
Nuts and Seeds		
Peanuts	1 ounce	4.9
Vegetables		
Asparagus	½ cup	1.5
Grains		
Wheat germ	1 ounce	1.5
Rice, brown	½ cup	1.2
Noodles, enriched	½ cup	1.0
Rice, white, enriched	½ cup	1.0
Bread, enriched	1 slice	0.7
Milk and Milk Products		
Cottage cheese	½ cup	2.6
Milk	1 cup	1.9

Vitamin B$_6$

Food	Vitamin B$_6$	
	Amount	**mg**
Meats		
Liver	3 ounces	0.8
Salmon	3 ounces	0.7
Other fish	3 ounces	0.6
Chicken	3 ounces	0.4
Ham	3 ounces	0.4
Hamburger	3 ounces	0.4
Veal	3 ounces	0.4
Pork	3 ounces	0.3
Beef	3 ounces	0.2
Eggs		
Egg	1	0.3
Legumes		
Split peas	½ cup	0.6
Dried beans, cooked	½ cup	0.4
Fruits		
Banana	1	0.6
Avocado	½	0.4
Watermelon	1 cup	0.3
Vegetables		
Turnip greens	½ cup	0.7
Brussels sprouts	½ cup	0.4
Potato	1	0.2
Sweet potato	½ cup	0.2
Carrots	½ cup	0.2
Peas	½ cup	0.1

Folate

Food	Folate	
	Amount	**mcg**
Vegetables		
Navy beans	½ cup	128
Asparagus	½ cup	120
Brussels sprouts	½ cup	116
Black-eyed peas	½ cup	102
Spinach, cooked	½ cup	99
Romaine lettuce	1 cup	86
Lima beans	½ cup	71
Peas	½ cup	70
Collard greens, cooked	½ cup	56
Sweet potato	½ cup	43
Broccoli	½ cup	43
Fruits		
Cantaloupe	¼ whole	100
Orange juice	1 cup	87
Orange	1	59
Grains★		
Breakfast cereals	1 cup	100–400
Oatmeal	½ cup	97
Wheat germ	¼ cup	80
Wild rice	½ cup	37

★ Refined grain products such as bread, white rice, and pasta are fortified with folic acid and provide approximately 40 mcg folate per serving.

Vitamin B$_{12}$

Food	Vitamin B$_{12}$	
	Amount	**mcg**
Meats		
Liver	3 ounces	6.8
Trout	3 ounces	3.6
Beef	3 ounces	2.2
Clams	½ cup	2.0
Crab	3 ounces	1.8
Lamb	3 ounces	1.8
Tuna	½ cup	1.8
Veal	3 ounces	1.7
Hamburger, regular	3 ounces	1.5
Milk and Milk Products		
Skim milk	1 cup	1.0
Milk	1 cup	0.9
Yogurt	1 cup	0.8
Cottage cheese	½ cup	0.7
American cheese	1 ounce	0.2
Cheddar cheese	1 ounce	0.2
Eggs		
Egg	1	0.6

B. Minerals

Calcium

Food	Calcium Amount	mg
Milk and Milk Products		
Yogurt, low-fat	1 cup	415
Yogurt with fruit, low-fat	1 cup	315
Milk, skim	1 cup	300
Milk, 1% fat	1 cup	300
Milk, 2% fat	1 cup	298
Milk, whole	1 cup	288
Swiss cheese	1 ounce	270
Cheddar cheese	1 ounce	205
Frozen yogurt	1 cup	200
Cream soup	1 cup	186
Pudding	½ cup	185
Ice cream	1 cup	180
Ice milk	1 cup	180
American cheese	1 ounce	175
Custard	½ cup	150
Cottage cheese	½ cup	70
Cottage cheese, low-fat	½ cup	69
Vegetables		
Spinach, cooked	½ cup	122
Collard greens, cooked	½ cup	110
Kale	½ cup	47
Broccoli	½ cup	36
Legumes		
Tofu	½ cup	260
Dried beans, cooked	½ cup	60
Lima beans	½ cup	40
Other		
Calcium-fortified orange juice	1 cup	100

Phosphorus

Food	Phosphorus Amount	mg
Milk and Milk Products		
Yogurt	1 cup	327
Milk, skim	1 cup	250
Milk, whole	1 cup	250
Cottage cheese	½ cup	150
American cheese	1 ounce	130
Meats		
Pork	3 ounces	275
Hamburger	3 ounces	165
Tuna	3 ounces	162
Lobster	3 ounces	125
Chicken	3 ounces	120
Nuts and Seeds		
Sunflower seeds	¼ cup	319
Peanuts	¼ cup	141
Pine nuts	¼ cup	106
Peanut butter	1 tablespoon	61
Grains		
Bran flakes	1 cup	180
Shredded wheat	2 large biscuits	81
Whole wheat bread	1 slice	52
Vegetables		
Potato	1 medium	101
Corn	½ cup	73
Peas	½ cup	70
French fries	½ cup	61
Broccoli	½ cup	54

Magnesium

Food	Magnesium Amount	mg
Legumes		
Lentils, cooked	½ cup	134
Split peas, cooked	½ cup	134
Tofu	½ cup	130
Nuts		
Peanuts	¼ cup	247
Cashews	¼ cup	93
Almonds	¼ cup	80
Grains		
Bran buds	1 cup	240
Wild rice, cooked	½ cup	119
Breakfast cereal, fortified	1 cup	85
Wheat germ	2 tablespoons	45
Vegetables		
Bean sprouts	½ cup	98
Black-eyed peas	½ cup	58
Spinach, cooked	½ cup	48
Lima beans	½ cup	32
Milk and Milk Products		
Milk	1 cup	30
Cheddar cheese	1 ounce	8
American cheese	1 ounce	6
Meats		
Chicken	3 ounces	25
Beef	3 ounces	20
Pork	3 ounces	20

Iron

Food	Iron Amount	mg
Meats and Dried Beans		
Liver	3 ounces	7.5
Round steak	3 ounces	3.0
Hamburger, lean	3 ounces	3.0
Baked beans	½ cup	3.0
Pork	3 ounces	2.7
White beans	½ cup	2.7
Soybeans	½ cup	2.5
Pork and beans	½ cup	2.3
Fish	3 ounces	1.0
Chicken	3 ounces	1.0
Grains		
Breakfast cereal, iron-fortified	1 cup	8.0 (4–18)
Oatmeal, fortified	1 cup	8.0
Bagel	1	1.7
English muffin	1	1.6
Rye bread	1 slice	1.0
Whole wheat bread	1 slice	0.8
White bread	1 slice	0.6
Fruits		
Prune juice	6 ounces	7.0
Apricots, dried	½ cup	2.5
Prunes	5 medium	2.0
Raisins	¼ cup	1.3
Plums	3 medium	1.1
Vegetables		
Spinach, cooked	½ cup	2.3
Lima beans	½ cup	2.2
Black-eyed peas	½ cup	1.7
Peas	½ cup	1.6
Asparagus	½ cup	1.5

Zinc

| | Zinc | |
Food	Amount	mg
Meats		
Liver	3 ounces	4.6
Beef	3 ounces	4.0
Crab	½ cup	3.5
Lamb	3 ounces	3.5
Turkey ham	3 ounces	2.5
Pork	3 ounces	2.4
Chicken	3 ounces	2.0
Legumes		
Dried beans, cooked	½ cup	1.0
Split peas, cooked	½ cup	0.9
Grains		
Breakfast cereal, fortified	1 cup	1.5–4.0
Wheat germ	2 tablespoons	2.4
Rice, brown	1 cup	1.2
Oatmeal	1 cup	1.2
Bran flakes	1 cup	1.0
Rice, white	1 cup	0.8
Nuts and Seeds		
Pecans	¼ cup	2.0
Cashews	¼ cup	1.8
Sunflower seeds	¼ cup	1.7
Peanut butter	2 tablespoons	0.9
Milk and Milk Products		
Cheddar cheese	1 ounce	1.1
Milk, whole	1 cup	0.9
American cheese	1 ounce	0.8

Selenium

| | Selenium | |
Food	Amount	mg
Seafood		
Lobster	3 ounces	66
Tuna	3 ounces	60
Shrimp	3 ounces	54
Oysters	3 ounces	48
Fish	3 ounces	40
Meats		
Liver	3 ounces	56
Ham	3 ounces	29
Beef	3 ounces	22
Bacon	3 ounces	21
Chicken	3 ounces	18
Lamb	3 ounces	14
Veal	3 ounces	10
Eggs		
Egg	1 medium	37

Sodium

Food	Sodium	
	Amount	mg
Miscellaneous		
Salt	1 teaspoon	2,132
Dill pickle	1 (4½ ounces)	1,930
Sea salt	1 teaspoon	1,716
Chicken broth	1 cup	1,571
Ravioli, canned	1 cup	1,065
Spaghetti with sauce, canned	1 cup	955
Baking soda	1 teaspoon	821
Beef broth	1 cup	782
Gravy	¼ cup	720
Italian dressing	2 tablespoons	720
Pretzels	5 (1 ounce)	500
Green olives	5	465
Pizza with cheese	1 wedge	455
Soy sauce	1 teaspoon	444
Meats		
Corned beef	3 ounces	808
Ham	3 ounces	800
Fish, canned	3 ounces	735
Meatloaf	3 ounces	555
Sausage	3 ounces	483
Hot dog	1	477
Fish, smoked	3 ounces	444

Potassium

| | Potassium | |
Food	Amount	mg
Vegetables		
Potato	1 medium	780
Winter squash	½ cup	327
Tomato	1 medium	300
Celery	1 stalk	270
Carrots	1 medium	245
Broccoli	½ cup	205
Fruits		
Avocado	½ medium	680
Banana	1 medium	440
Orange juice	6 ounces	375
Raisins	¼ cup	370
Watermelon	2 cups	315
Prunes	4 large	300
Meats		
Fish	3 ounces	500
Hamburger	3 ounces	480
Lamb	3 ounces	382
Pork	3 ounces	335
Chicken	3 ounces	208
Grains		
Bran buds	1 cup	1,080
Bran flakes	1 cup	248
Raisin bran	1 cup	242
Wheat flakes	1 cup	96
Milk and Milk Products		
Yogurt	1 cup	531
Milk, skim	1 cup	400
Milk, whole	1 cup	370
Other		
Salt substitutes	1 teaspoon	1,300–2,378

Iodine

	Iodine	
Food	**Amount**	**mcg**
Salt		
Iodized salt	1 teaspoon	400
Fish and Seafood		
Haddock	3 ounces	125
Cod	3 ounces	87
Shrimp	3 ounces	30
Other		
Bread	1 ounce	35–142
Cottage cheese	½ cup	50
Egg	1	22
Cheddar cheese	1 ounce	17

The iodine content of foods varies based on growing conditions and use of iodine in breads and in cleaning food manufacturing equipment. Fish and seaweeds such as kelp and nori are generally good sources.

⌒ Appendix B ⌒

Converting to Metrics

VOLUME MEASUREMENT CONVERSIONS

U.S.	Metric
¼ teaspoon	1.25 ml
½ teaspoon	2.5 ml
¾ teaspoon	3.75 ml
1 teaspoon	5 ml
1 tablespoon	15 ml
¼ cup	62.5 ml
½ cup	125 ml
¾ cup	187.5 ml
1 cup	250 ml

WEIGHT CONVERSION MEASUREMENTS

U.S.	Metric
1 ounce	28.4 g
8 ounces	227.5 g
16 ounces (1 pound)	455 g

COOKING TEMPERATURE CONVERSIONS

Fahrenheit	Celsius/Centigrade
Fahrenheit established 0°F as the stabilized temperature when equal amounts of ice, water, and salt are mixed.	0°C and 100°C are arbitrarily placed at the melting and boiling points of water and are standard to the metric system.

To convert temperatures in Fahrenheit to Celsius, use this formula:

$$C = (F - 32) \times 0.5555$$

So, for example, if you are baking at 350°F and want to know that temperature in Celsius, use this calculation:

$$C = (350 - 32) \times 0.5555 = 176.66°C$$

⌒ References ⌒

Chapter 1

Ahima, R. S. "Body fat, leptin, and hypothalamic amenorrhea." *New England Journal of Medicine* 351:959–62, 2004.

Brown, J. E., et al. *Nutrition Through the Lifecycle*, 2d ed. Belmont, CA: Wadsworth/Thomson Publishing Company, 2005.

Brown, J. E., and E. S. B. Kahn. "Maternal nutrition and the outcome of pregnancy: A renaissance in research." *Clinics in Perinatology* 24:433–49, 1997.

Caballero, B. *New England Journal of Medicine* 52:1514–16, 2005.

Cziezel, A. E. "Preconceptional folic acid-containing multivitamin supplementation." *European Journal of Obstetrics, Gynecology, and Reproductive Biology* 78:151–61, 1998.

Dietary Supplements. nlm.gov/medlineplus/dietary supplements.html, 2005.

Ehrmann, D. A. "Polycystic ovary syndrome." *New England Journal of Medicine* 352:1223–36, 2005.

Eskenazi, B. et al. "Antioxidants boost sperm count and motility." *Human Reproduction* 20:1006–12, 2005.

Food and Nutrition Board, Institute of Medicine, National Academies of Science. *Dietary Reference Intakes*. Washington, DC: National Academies Press, 1997–2004.

Hoeger, K. M., et al. "Weight loss restores ovulation in obese women with PCOS." *Fertility and Sterility* 82:421–29, 2004.

Sperling, M. A. "Prematurity—a window of opportunity?" *New England Journal of Medicine* 351:2229–31, 2003.

Wong, W. Y., et al. "Male factor subfertility: Possible causes and the impact of nutritional factors." *Fertility and Sterility* 73:435–42, 2000.

Chapter 2

Brown, J. E. *Nutrition Now*, 4th ed. Belmont, CA: Wadsworth/Thomson Publishing Company, 2005.

Food and Nutrition Board, Institute of Medicine, National Academies of Science. *Dietary Reference Intakes*. Washington, DC: National Academies Press, 1997–2004.

Foster-Powell, K., et al. "International table of glycemic index and glycemic load values." *American Journal of Clinical Nutrition* 76:5–56, 2002.

Chapter 3

Brown, J. E., and E. S. B. Kahn. "Maternal nutrition and the outcome of pregnancy: A renaissance in research." *Clinics in Perinatology* 24:433–49, 1997.

Brown, J.E., et al. *Nutrition Through the Lifecycle*, 2d ed. Belmont, CA: Wadsworth/Thomson Publishing Company, 2005.

Brown, J. E., et al. "Predictors of red cell folate level in women attempting pregnancy." *Journal of the American Medical Association* 277:548–52, 1997.

Dolan, S. M. "Isotretinion and pregnancy: A continued risk for birth defects." *Medscape Ob/Gyn & Women's Health*, medscape.com, 9(2), 2004.

Fall, C. H. D., et al. "Micronutrients and fetal growth." *Journal of Nutrition* 133:17475–565, 2003.

Gillman, M. W. "Developmental origins of health and disease." *New England Journal of Medicine* 353:1848–50, 2005

McCann, J. C., and B. N. Ames. "Is docosahexaenoic acid required for development of normal brain function? An overview of evidence from cognitive and behavioral tests in humans and animals." *American Journal of Clinical Nutrition* 82:281–95, 2005.

"Position of the American Dietetic Association: Nutrition and lifestyle for a healthy pregnancy outcome." *Journal of the American Dietetics Association* 102:1479–90, 2002.

Scholl, T. O. "Iron status during pregnancy: Setting the stage for mother and infant." *American Journal of Clinical Nutrition* 81(suppl)1218S–22S, 2005.

Chapter 4

Brown, J. E., et al. *Nutrition Through the Lifecycle*, 2d ed. Belmont, CA: Wadsworth/Thomson Publishing Company, 2005.

Institute of Medicine, National Academy of Sciences. *Nutrition During Pregnancy*, Washington, DC: National Academy of Sciences Press, 1990.

Chapter 5

Allen, L. H. "Multiple micronutrients in pregnancy and lactation: An overview." *American Journal of Clinical Nutrition* 81(suppl):1206S–12S, 2005.

Belew, C. "Herbs and the childbearing woman." *Journal of Nurse-Midwifery* 44:231–52, 1999.

Brown, J. E., and M. Carlson. "Nutrition and twin pregnancy." *Journal of the American Dietetic Association* 100:343-8, 2000.

Brown, J. E., et al. "Prepregnancy weight status, prenatal weight gain, and the outcome of term twin gestations." *American Journal of Obstetrics and Gynecology* 162:182–86, 1990.

Institute of Medicine, National Academy of Sciences. *Nutrition During Pregnancy*. Washington, DC: National Academy of Sciences Press, 1990.

Lantz, M. E., et al. "Maternal weight gain patterns and birth weight outcome in twin gestation." *Obstetrics and Gynecology* 87:551–56, 1996.

McCory, M. A. "The role of diet and exercise in postpartum weight management." *Nutrition Today* 35:175–82, 2000.

Chapter 6

Brown, J. E. "Weight gain during pregnancy: What is optimal?" *Clinical Nutrition* 7:181–190, 1988.

Brown J. E., and E. S. B. Kahn. "Maternal and nutrition and the outcome of pregnancy: A renaissance in research." *Clinics in Perinatology* 24:433–49, 1997.

Brown, J. E., et al. "Variation in newborn size according to pregnancy weight change by trimester." *American Journal of Clinical Nutrition* 76:205–9, 2002.

Institute of Medicine, National Academy of Sciences. *Nutrition During Pregnancy*, Washington, DC: National Academy of Sciences Press, 1990.

Keppel, K. G., and S. M. Taffel. "Pregnancy-related weight gain and retention: Implications of the 1990 Institute of Medicine Guidelines." *American Journal of Public Health* 83:1100–3, 1993.

Rothman, K. J., et al. "Teratogenicity of high vitamin A intake." *New England Journal of Medicine* 333:1369–73, 1995.

Chapter 7

"Exercise during pregnancy." medscape.com, 2005.

Johnson, K. "Pregnancy exercise recommendations growing more liberal." *Medscape Ob/Gyn & Women's Health*, medscape.com, 8(2), 2003.

Chapter 8

Brown J. E., et al. *Nutrition Through the Lifecycle*, 2d ed. Belmont, CA: Wadsworth/Thomson Publishing Company, 2005.

Catalano, P. M. et al. "Gestational diabetes and insulin resistance: Role in short- and long-term implications for mother and fetus." *Journal of Nutrition* 133:16745–835, 2003.

Cogswell M. E., et al. "Iron supplementation during pregnancy, anemia, and birth weight: A randomized controlled trial." *American Journal of Clinical Nutrition* 78:773–81, 2003.

Crowther, C. A. et al. "Effect of treatment of gestational diabetes on pregnancy outcomes." *New England Journal of Medicine* 352:2477–86, 2005.

Institute of Medicine, National Academy of Sciences. *Nutrition During Pregnancy.* Washington, DC: National Academy of Sciences Press, 1990.

Jovanovic-Peterson, L., and C. M. Peterson. "Exercise and the nutritional management of diabetes during pregnancy." *Obstetrics and Gynecology Clinics of North America* 23:75–86, 1996.

Makrides, M. et al. "Efficacy and tolerability of low-dose iron supplements during pregnancy: A randomized controlled trial." *American Journal of Clinical Nutrition* 78:145–53, 2003.

Roodenburg, A. J. C. "Iron supplements during pregnancy." *European Journal of Obstetrics, Gynecology, and Reproductive Biology* 61:65–71, 1995.

Vutyavanich, T., et al. "Pyridoxine for nausea and vomiting of pregnancy: A randomized double-blind, placebo-controlled trial." *American Journal of Obstetrics and Gynecology* 73:881–84, 1995.

Chapter 9

Birch, E. E., et al. "Visual maturation of term infants fed long-chain polyunsaturated fatty acid-supplemented or control formula for 12 months." *American Journal of Clinical Nutrition* 81:871–79, 2005.

Butte, N., et al. "The Start Healthy Feeding Guidelines for Infants and Toddlers." *Journal of the American Dietetic Association* 104:422–54, 2004.

Mangels, A. R., et al. "Considerations in the planning of vegan diets: Infants." *Journal of the American Dietetic Association* 1–1:670–77, 2001.

Satter, E. "The feeding relationship: Problems and interventions." *Journal of Pediatrics* 117:5181–89, 1990.

Story, M., and J. E. Brown. "Do young children instinctively know what to eat? The studies of Clara Davis revisited." *New England Journal of Medicine* 316:103–6, 1987.

Chapter 10

Allen, L. H. "Multiple micronutrients in pregnancy and lactation: an overview." *American Journal of Clinical Nutrition* 81(suppl):1206S–12S, 2005.

American Academy of Pediatrics. "Breastfeeding and the use of human milk." *Pediatrics* 100:1035–39, 1997.

Fidel-Rimon, O., et al. "Breast-feeding multiples." *Seminars in Neonatology* 7:231–9, 2002.

Institute of Medicine, National Academy of Sciences. *Nutrition During Lactation*. Washington, DC: National Academy Press, 1991.

Rogan, W. G. "Pollutants in breast milk." *Archives of Pediatric and Adolescent Medicine* 150:981–90, 1996.

Strode, M. A., et al. "Effects of short-term caloric restriction on lactational performance of well-nourished women." *Acta Paediatrica Scandinavia* 75:222–29, 1986.

⌒ Additional Resources ⌒

Chapter 1

fns.usda.gov

USDA's homepage for food and nutrition information, with links to the U.S. Dietary Guidelines, MyPyramid food guide, and general information about nutrition

nutrition.gov

A guide to reliable information on nutrition and health

nlm.nih.gov

The National Library of Medicine's homepage, with links to excellent information on nutrition, fertility, pregnancy, breast-feeding, and infant nutrition

nccaom.org and medicalacupuncture.org

Check out alternative care providers and alternative care for infertility through the Commission for Acupuncture and Oriental Medicine, the Physician's Acupuncture Group. Or see *Fertility and Sterility* 81:93–98 and 1578–84, 2004.

obgyn.net/PCOS/PCOS.asp

PCOS chat room

nlm.nih.gov/medlineplus/infertility.html

The National Library of Medicine provides high-quality information on infertility; access other health topics by changing the last term in the address.

ncbi.nlm.nih.gov/pubmed
Enter a search term and find full-length articles and abstracts on fertility and early pregnancy topics

clinicaltrials.gov
Search "infertility" and find a list of ongoing and planned research studies by the National Institutes of Health. You, your partner, or others you know may qualify for a trial.

glutenfree.com or 800-291-8386
Source for gluten-free ingredients and products

Fenster, Carol, *Wheat-Free Recipes and Menus*. NY: Penguin, 2004.

Hagman, Betty, *The Gluten-Free Gourmet and the Gluten-Free Cook's Comfort Food*. NY: Henry Holt, 2004.

Chapter 2

nutrition.gov
A guide to reliable information on nutrition and health. MyPyramid.gov homepage for the 2005 MyPyramid food guide. Links to "Analyze My Food Intake," sample menus, and physical activity guides.

Chapter 3

pregnancy.webmd.com
Go to the pregnancy health center to access week-by-week information about your pregnancy and a due date calculator.

Chapter 4

fightbac.org, cdc.gov/foodsafety
Food safety resources

vegetarian.net, vrg.org
Vegetarian diets and pregnancy information

epa.gov/ost/fish
Check local fish advisories here.

Chapter 5

nccam.nih.gov, http://dietary-supplements.info.nih.gov, http://ods
.od.nih.gov/index.aspx
These sites lead to information on dietary and herbal supplements and pregnancy.

Chapter 8

mayoclinic.com, WebMd.com, medlineplus.gov
Use these web sites to learn about clinical conditions in pregnancy.

Chapter 9

nal.usda.gov/fnic/wicdbase
Provides information on the Women, Infant, Children (WIC)
program and eligibility standards

cdc.gov/growthcharts
Get a copy of the Centers for Disease Control infant and child
growth charts from this site.

Chapter 10

nlm.nih.gov/medlineplus/breastfeeding.html, cdc.gov/breastfeeding,
aap.org, breastfeeding.org, lalecheleague.org.
These sites provide breast-feeding information and referrals to
support groups or to lactation consultants.

⇒ Index ⇐

Page numbers in **bold** refer to recipes.

⤳ About the Author ⤲

Judith E. Brown, R.D., M.P.H., Ph.D., is Professor Emerita of Nutrition at the University of Minnesota's School of Public Health and the Department of Obstetrics and Gynecology. She came to the University of Minnesota after completing a Ph.D. in Nutrition at Florida State University and an M.P.H. in Public Health Nutrition at the University of Michigan. The author of over one hundred scientific publications, Dr. Brown is a leading researcher in maternal nutrition. She now provides continuing education in preconception and prenatal nutrition to health-care professionals nationally and serves as a consultant to pharmaceutical and food companies and to government agencies. Dr. Brown was awarded the March of Dimes Agnes Higgins Award in Maternal Nutrition and is a past chair of the Women's and Reproductive Nutrition Practice Group of the American Dietetic Association. She is the author of two leading college textbooks on nutrition: *Nutrition Now* and *Nutrition Through the Lifecycle*.